The Small Business Guide to **Marketing, Lead Generation and Sales**

Martyn Kinch

Copyright

ISBN: 978-1-291-54693-4

Published by Martyn Kinch

About the Author

I have been selling products, services and intangibles since I was 21, over 34 years ago. In that time, I have learnt an awful lot along the way and now I want to pass it on to you.

This book is based on my experience of building a number of businesses from nothing, creating the illusion of being bigger than we were, getting prospects to come to me and taking on, and beating, the competition.

Whether it was selling brass on a market stall, importing clothes, creating a perfumery, selling computers or distributing software, I have learnt how a holistic approach to selling can make you smarter than the competition and get your potential customers to come to you.

This book is also based on my experience of harnessing current technology and of thinking about and adapting to how the new generation of potential customers buy. We look at everything from utilising social media, to marketing and selling, search engines, email, exhibitions and much more.

The knowledge I have gained over the years, I will show you how with some simple guidelines, you too can bring together the many threads that will make you, your company, product or service, number one in your market and give you the 'edge'.

Dedication

This book is dedicated to my family.

Heather, for her dedication, wisdom, and bringing some structure to what I do.

Victoria and James, our children, for accepting that business was a part of our everyday lives and my apologies to them for every holiday that always combined a little bit of business and, of course, just when they thought it was time to relax, finding a new idea and starting again …

Forward

"Martyn is an approachable and understanding individual, who is a real expert in the sales process, finding the "edge", and making things happen in a positive and entrepreneurial way.

With all his knowledge and experience, Martyn has a great skill in being able to relate to others' business needs, aspirations, or problems, and is a master at being able to ask the right questions, probe in the right areas, and help guide decision making in a balanced and manageable way.

A great guy to work with!"

Jonny Cowan,
Assistant CEO, Sport England

"Martyn is an amazing person to work with. I had the chance to work with him as a business partner and later as an employee in his division.

I'm really impressed by his skills of managing large-sized opportunities with clients worldwide.

He's very good at building and maintaining long-lasting business relationships.

He excels in providing the best to his clients, as well as his team.

Martyn is very well respected by his peers and those he leads.

I would recommend Martyn highly, and especially applaud his ability to always get the best out of any given situation.

He is a seasoned professional and very knowledgeable in his field."

Kenneth Baek,
Country Manager for Scandinavia

"Martyn is the most knowledgeable man I have ever had the pleasure of working with/ for.

He has an absolute wealth of knowledge within our industry and his ideas and foresight are second to none. Martyn is a joy to work with and makes coming to work a real pleasure."

Paula Gower,
Telesales Supervisor

"Having worked with Martyn for over 13 years, I have been very fortunate in witnessing a master at work.

He is both innovative and passionate about everything he does, and this is reflected in the amazing results that he delivers year on year.

He certainly believes in leading by example, and is a true professional in everything that he does."

Denise Maxfield,
Custom Relations Director

"Martyn is a highly respected professional in the industry, reflecting his long role as one of the 'Founding Fathers' of ITIL and PRINCE2 Training.

More than that, he is a true gentleman whose courtesy and humour support clients and colleagues alike. It's a real pleasure to work with him."

Annelise Savill,
Publisher, Van Haren Publishing

"Martyn is a very experienced senior international executive.

I have had the pleasure of working with Martyn in meeting the needs of the New Zealand market.

"Thoroughly professional and at home in meeting the requirements for proposals of significant value, or talking one-on-one with individual decision makers.

Martyn's achievements in developing new operations in Australia, New Zealand, South Africa, Oman, Dubai, Abu Dhabi, Qatar, Denmark and the USA, as well as his division's ability to meet demand in 90+ countries, is proof of his international business abilities."

Murray Wills,
Owner, Maxsys Limited, New Zealand

"Martyn is a very commercially astute and personable individual. He is highly thought of, not only by me, but also by his colleagues and fellow industry professionals.

I would not hesitate to recommend him to anyone looking for someone who can make a positive impact on their business."

Nick Bate,
Co-founder/Director, Blue Eskimo Solutions Ltd

"Martyn has a unique blend of entrepreneurial flair and ideas, coupled with an understanding of people and an ability to motivate that produces outstanding results."

Malcolm Farrar,
Chairman of The Manchester Footdown Group

"I have known Martyn for many years. We have worked together on many projects and shared many of the same customers.

What I respect the most about Martyn, is his positive, honest approach to providing customers with solutions that actually meet their needs. Highly recommend him.

He will always go the extra mile to make a difference!"

Eddie Borup,
Director, Ibp Solutions

"Martyn brings such a positive energy to his work. He is a pleasure to work with and always has valuable insights to offer.

I have seen Martyn at work over too many years to admit to, and he has maintained honesty, integrity, professionalism, enthusiasm and expertise throughout.

My experience is that Martyn listens to clients and understands their needs. This means he is able to identify solutions which fit perfectly to their circumstances.

I have learnt over the years that if Martyn recommends something, it is worth listening to him."

Una Mcgarvie (FCIPD, MAPM, MCMI, MBCS)

"I have had the pleasure of supporting Martyn in business over the past 15 years.

Martyn is one of the most professional and gifted people I have worked with over the years.

There are people in life that you know will be very successful, as they have a gift and a great respect for those they work with and the values they have in life."

Heather Carter,
Founder, Smart Contact Ltd, Cheshire

"In my dealings with Martyn, I have always found him to be very professional and pleasant to work with.

I found Martyn likes to find a solution that is beneficial to both parties and will drive at ensuring that this is achieved.

I would personally be very happy to work with Martyn again."

Simon Turner,
Executive Director, Foster-Melliar South Africa

"Over the last 10 years, and in many different roles, Martyn has been, without doubt ,the most intuitive, innovative and capable individual that I have had the good fortune to work with."

Eddie Kilkelly,
Managing Director, ILX Group PLC

"Throughout my dealings with Martyn, I found him to be not only a thorough professional, but also exceptionally easy to work with.

He was always approachable and was able to offer a much greater level of insight and direction to any project than I would deem usual.

I would be happy to work with Martyn again on any project."

Jamie Beeston,
Owner, Megellen Consulting

Acknowledgements

My thanks and gratitude to the many people that have provided me with support and guidance over the years.

In particular, I would like to thank Tom for his advice and patience, Kim, our accountant, for keeping me on the straight and narrow, and my very close friend Zhaun, for making me aspire to want more and for the manic energy he brought with him.

Nothing rarely happens without a great team, and I would like to acknowledge all the people I have worked with over the years; my absolute trust in them, and theirs in me, helped us achieve the near impossible.

How to Use this Book

To help you get the most out of this book, I have provided examples, tips, resources, references and a glossary.

The **examples** are drawn, for the most part from my own experiences and are set out in bold.

The **tips** come from my wife, my colleagues in business as well as from me.

I have also tried to provide as many **resources and references** as possible to enable you to extend your research; you will find these at the end of sections or at the end of chapters.

The **glossary** aims to explain the terms that are common currency within the sales, marketing and social media world.

I have started a **blog** to run alongside this book, and I would really welcome any feedback, or ideas that we can develop into an updated book later in the year. All contributions will be acknowledged and thankfully received.

Please go to **martynkinch.blogspot.com** for more information, updates and details on how my next new business is going.

Contents

STEP 8 150

SELL LIKE A PRO 150

Introduction

"Holistic adj.: Emphasizing the importance of the whole and the interdependence of its parts."

I like business books, particularly books on selling. When I'm waiting around at an airport or railway station, you'll find me scouring the business section for all the latest titles. It has always struck me though, that whilst I can find any number of books on selling or marketing or getting-rich-quick, I have never found a book that showed start-up companies how to succeed in tough markets.

For to be successful in that environment, you need to pull together all the threads of your business so that you make yourself, your company and your product or service so attractive that customers will want to search you out, as much you want to search for them.

The way to achieve this is to consider, when developing your business or product, all the tools and techniques available. Then you need to bring them together to construct a lead-generation machine and create the impression that you are a large and mature organisation, in order to succeed in today's world of fast-changing markets and technologies. In other words, you've got to think holistic.

We know, because we did, and it paid off. Using the approach outlined in this book, and the experience gained from building several successful businesses, we took on the competition, went international and became the number one player in our chosen markets. Not bad, when you consider that we started in our back bedroom, and did it all without borrowing a penny. What's more to the point here, is that we're sure you can do this too, and this book will explain how.

STEP 1

FOLLOW BUSINESS RULES

Step 1

"A journey of a thousand miles must begin with a single step."
~ Lao Tsu

Many years ago, I realised that to sell services or products, you need to understand the potential customer you're trying to catch.

One of the common themes running through this book is that understanding your potential customer is even more important than your service, product or company. People around you will tell you what they think about everything, but I learned long ago that only one person's thoughts matter, and that is the person who is going to buy from you.

Understanding Customer Buying Methods

To do that, you need to work at it. It's too easy to assume that you know what your customer wants and easy to forget, in this fast moving world that we live in, that what they wanted last month may not be the same next month. Instead, you need to stay in touch at ground floor level, regardless of the size of your business, for often it's when you start putting layers of people between you and your customer, that you lose touch with your potential market.

So, when I started out in my business I embarked on a little customer research project, talking to individuals and corporate customers after purchase, either on the phone or in person, or at our seminars. I asked why they bought from us instead of from our competitors and why they chose one product over another. What I discovered was that whilst some buyers bought on a whim, most based the purchase decision on information - about the company and the product or service - that they had gleaned from different sources.

Different Buyers

The technical buyer would pay particular attention to reviews and reinforce their decision by looking for technical information using tools such as Google, YouTube and online forums. The corporate buyer would use Google, but also be influenced by LinkedIn, your corporate website, your articles and your company's general presence in the marketplace. All buyers could be swayed by things such as testimonials, White Papers that showed company expertise, trade advertising, exhibition presence, books published, accreditations gained and memberships of professional bodies.

So, what it comes down to is this: if we want to succeed in tough markets, we need to be wherever any of those buyers go to look for the information that they use to help them make their purchasing decisions. To do that, we need to adopt a holistic approach to our company, products and services. That way, regardless of the buyer and requirements, they will find us, and we will find them.

Based on this research, I have given myself one simple objective that I set out to achieve every time we create a product or service or enter a new market: when a potential prospect looks for a product or service like mine, I want to ensure I am one of the top three companies that they consider.

Quite a simple, powerful, and you might think, unrealistic statement, because to achieve that goal - your goal - we have to ensure we cover every single angle that a potential buyer would look at. It is, nevertheless, a goal that is eminently achievable.

Example

For a time, I ran a company that specialised in distributing CD related training which we sourced from the USA. The subject matter was training in C and C++, which, at the time, was a popular programming language.

I was finding it difficult to get the sales momentum going, and as this was many years ago, the web was still growing and social media hadn't started in the way that it has today. I decided to go along to a technical it exhibition as a visitor and noticed that one of the busiest stands was giving away a magazine with an attached CD on the cover, and realised that our potential customers used magazines to help them make their purchase decisions.

I took the details of the magazine, rang its editor to see what it would take for me to have a sample of my cd material on the cover CD, and before I knew it, they were very happy to consider it. So we created a stand-alone part of the course that a potential prospect could run direct from the magazine CD, and try out our training solution.

It took three months for the edition that had our details on the cover CD to arrive, but when it did, sales and enquiries took off. We then replicated it with the other magazines, offering free trial lessons and then once we had the route to the market, we took on further technical courses using the same formulae.

In any one month, our cd was on one or more magazine covers, from which we got some excellent reviews by the magazines themselves, which in turn, further boosted sales.

Within six months we were shipping hundreds of CDs a month all over the UK. By the end of the year my company was the largest provider of online technical C/C++ and java training in the UK.

All this came from researching my typical buyers and how they supported their purchasing decision. A process that I think can be replicated in any marketplace.

One of the best things that you can do, therefore, that will help you with the rest of this book, is to put yourself in your potential customer's place and think through: how they would find you? And what they would look for to reinforce the decision to buy from you?

At the same time, you should think about your competitors. As a new business, it's helpful to set your sights on a competitor that you want to emulate or beat. This can help you refine your approach and technique, as you will see throughout the book, and it will also help your potential customers understand who you are.

Martyn's Top Tips

- Know your customer.
- Find out how customers in your market buy.
- Know the different kinds of customers you have.
- Aim to be in the top three companies that potential customers in your marketplace consider.
- Target a competitor to give yourself a goal.

Keep It Simple

I have a favourite saying that I use in my business, that drives people nuts, but that works:

"If you can't draw it with a crayon then you can't sell it."

A little simplistic, I hear you say, but the principle is that you need to be able to describe your business, product or service in two or three words, in terms of what your potential customer might look for.

You may have different words for different parts of your business, but for each key area you should follow this principle to help brand you and the business.

Why do you need to do this? We live in a complex and changing world and it is tempting to develop complicated and convoluted methods to navigate through it when the opposite is true.

My experience has shown me that if you focus in on the three words, you will understand the business that you are in and reach your customer, so that you can establish your brand. I'll come back to an example of my crayon technique later, but first, I want to take you through a number of principles that will help you find those three little words.

The Zulu Principle

In my experience you can be really good, even world beating, at one thing. Try to be good at two things, however, and things start to get blurred; aim for three and you're likely to lose focus altogether.

Example

Imagine you have to sell the complete, A through to Z range of stationery items to potential customers. Even after several weeks, it is unlikely that you will have become an expert in any one item, but highly probable that you will have found yourself competing with every other stationery seller knocking on customers' doors.

Now, imagine you have to sell a single model of biro. That's it, nothing else. Within weeks, and after some research, you will probably have become one of the most knowledgeable biro salespeople in the business. As a result, when you did go about selling your biro, you would do it with a passion and expertise that would persuade people to buy from you. That is the Zulu Principle.

I learnt this from Jim Slater's great book of that title. He says that one day his wife read an article on Zulus in the Reader's Digest.

From that point on, she knew more about Zulus than he did. If she had then gone on to borrow a book from the local library she would probably have known more than most people in the county. If after that, she had visited South Africa and spent six months studying all the available literature on Zulus and stayed in a Zulu Kraal, she would probably have become one of the leading authorities on the subject in Great Britain, if not the world.

Jim Slater's point is that Zulu history and culture are clearly defined and narrow areas of knowledge on which his wife would have spent a considerable amount of time and effort, thus making her an expert. He then goes on to explain how the Zulu Principle can be used in financial markets by concentrating knowledge and focus.

It was a light-bulb moment for me. Now, in every product or service I sell and every market I sell in, I find the Zulu Principle part and focus on that. Indeed, it is the basis of the strategy we will use to position your company so it is important that you get the concept.

Focus on your Product or Company

Over the years, I have come across many companies who really struggle to put into a few simple words what they do. This is because they are looking at the big picture. They should, instead, home-in on the close-up shot.

The trick is to find a key product, service or part of your company, get it tightly focused, 'productise' and simplify it to use it as an arrow to enter unnoticed into the market to get your first order. Use this tactic, and you might go under the purchasing radar because it falls below sign-off levels.

Or, you might find that you deal with a specialist buyer who has more time for you than the general buyer who gets hundreds of cold calls a day.

The end result is that, in a Trojan-Horse-style manoeuvre, you have established a trading record, small though it may be, which now makes it easier to up-sell and grow the account.

Make the Main Thing, the Main Thing

"The main thing is, to keep the main thing, the main thing, at all times." I saw Stephen Covey's powerful words on a customer's desk many years ago. It should be written large on every entrepreneur's wall. My business partner, Tom, certainly thought so sometimes: he would put it down in front of me every time I went in with a new idea or got bored with the one we were working on. It can happen to the best of us. You get your core idea and then before you know it, other ideas spin off it: new markets, new services and new products pop into your head; all seem great and you get enthusiastic and motivated by each one. Resist temptation! Maintain a laser-like focus on Stephen Covey's "main thing". Be the best at what you do, be the most knowledgeable, be the most skillful and you will be successful. Flit around like a butterfly, and you risk taking your eye off your core business and missing an opportunity.

Pareto's Law

The Pareto principle (also known as the 80-20 rule, the law of the vital few and the principle of factor sparsity) states that, for many events, roughly 80% of the effects come from 20% of the causes.
Business-management consultant, Joseph M. Juran, suggested the principle and named it after Italian economist, Vilfredo Pareto who, in 1906, observed that 80% of the land in Italy was owned by 20% of the population; he developed the principle to note that 20% of the pea pods in his garden contained 80% of the peas. Let me expand this into other areas.

I can confidently say, that I generally only need to understand 20% of a subject to get 80% of its benefits. I can also predict that while this book will not make you an expert on tweeting – there are plenty to do that – my book will, instead, give you a little enough of the right knowledge so that you end up in the top 20% of your marketplace.

Taking this a step further, it's a well-known common rule of thumb in business that 80% of your sales come from 20% of your clients. In fact, over the years I have found that the 80/20 rule has been a good way of measuring many aspects of your business. So chances are, that 80% of your revenue will come from 20% of your products; 20% of your sales staff will produce 80% of your revenue; 80% of your sales will come from 20% of your customers. It is not an exact science - and the ratio could be 70/30 - but it is a useful rule to bear in mind, in terms of directing your effort and money.

Pour Petrol on a Fire

What do you do when you have this 80/20 split in terms of revenue and product? Use the Pareto Principle to focus your activities. Or, as Steve Ballmer from Microsoft said, if he finds a fire – a high performing product, in his case - he pours petrol on it. If that is where the money is, that is where the effort goes. On the other hand, we all know the saying, "Too many eggs in one basket." None of us wants to become the company that is dependent on one major product or market, for we all know too well that things can go badly wrong if conditions change. Diversification is, therefore, important.

So what do you do? There is no simple answer; it is different for every business. You need to consider, devise and modify your strategy, based on your company and on the market. Once you have your strategy and product, then you need to keep an eye on trends and developments and find ways to reach the customer. This is where we go back to my crayon technique. As, drawing on all these principles, you can now come up with three words that will perfectly encapsulate the business that you are in.

Example

Imagine you're in the estate agent business. Property sales have stagnated, buyers are hard to find but you are trying to reach and sell to them. What are your little words? The first words you come up with might be: "house sales." Not bad, it tells people the type of property you're selling but there are a million companies out there with more money than you have, trying to make sure they are recognized for those words. You have got to be smarter and differentiate it more. So your next step could be to focus in on the geography and describe it by: *'House sales, Cheshire.'* or *'House sales, Nantwich.'*

Indeed, follow the rules in this book, provide a quality product and excellent service, and you will find it much easier to become the first choice for local people and the 'Largest estate agent in Nantwich' before expanding to other geographic locations using the same formula.

The example is fairly simple and you can refine it further, but you get my drift. For, once you focus down the message, it becomes much easier to come in the top 10 in internet searches, which means you are now on the first step of getting your brand established.

Martyn's Top Tips

- If you can't draw it with a crayon then you can't sell it.
- Try to describe your product in three words or less.
- Follow the Zulu Principle.
- Home in on one product if you have a range of products or services.
- The main thing is, is to keep the main thing, the main thing at all times.
- Remember Pareto's 80/20 Law.
- Pour petrol on a fire – if it looks as though you have hit a good market then go all out to dominate it.
- What would a potential customer type in a search engine to find you or your product?

References and Resources

Amazon search for Pareto's Law:
http://www.amazon.co.uk/s/ref=nb_sb_noss?url=search-alias%3Daps&field-keywords=pareto%27s+law

Amazon search for The Zulu Principle:
http://www.amazon.co.uk/s/ref=nb_sb_noss_1?url=search-alias%3Daps&field-keywords=the+zulu+principle&rh=i%3Aaps%2Ck%3Athe+zulu+principle.

STEP 2

BRAND YOUR IMAGE

Step 2

"Behaviour is the mirror in which everyone shows their image." ~ **Johann Wolfgang von Goethe**

Princeton University psychologists have discovered that we make up our minds about people within a tenth of a second. Think about it for a moment: that's one tenth of a second - one tenth of a second in which people have completely made up their mind about you. Image, or how people see you, therefore, is incalculably important. For after that tenth of a second, if you have made a bad start, you can only hope that they spend the rest of the time they are with you adjusting that view in a positive way. So, follow my tips below, and you will, hopefully, never need to worry about that.

Polish your Personal Image

Sounds a very obvious thing to do (I expect), but in my experience, it's the little obvious things that we sometimes forget, that can make all the difference. So avoid this pitfall and treat yourself and every area of your business as part of the product or service you are selling.

What you wear, what you use to demonstrate, what you write with, the way you sit, how you cross your legs, how you listen: they all say little things about you, your company and your product or service. Make sure they say the right things.

Beg, borrow, hire or invest, in the best dress, suit or outfit that is appropriate for the meeting, the people you are going meet, the relationship you want to have with them and the role you are going to play. Overdress, and you could look too slick; underdress, and you may lack polish. Look good and you will feel good. So before you go to your meeting, look at yourself in the mirror – would you or would your customer buy from you?

Brush Up your Company Image

First impressions are everything, as you have gathered by now, and that applies to what people hear as well as what they see. Potential customers form their views about your product and service from the moment someone answers your phone.

Make sure that whoever it is - answering service, partner, marketing director, receptionist - answers it professionally every single time. Sounds simple doesn't it? Honestly though, how often have you put the phone down to a company and felt that you had had a productive and satisfactory conversation with a nice organisation? Not as often as it should be, I'm sure, yet this simple and easy measure can make a considerable difference to your business.

Example

When we set up our office, we agreed the following: that we should all use the same introduction for answering the phone, that no phone should ring for more than six rings, if possible, that whoever answered the phone would own the call/question/action until it was handed over and that the call would be returned, regardless of who it was for. What a difference it made.

Simply being friendly to callers and ensuring someone got back to them, made their experience of dealing with us so much better. Not only did it improve our customer service, but it improved the sales process. Like I said: simple and effective.

Present a Good Front

When you're starting up a business, budgets are tight. But however tight they may be in that start-up period, always remember the image you are trying to create. When we set up our first company, we wanted our image to reflect our ability to deliver great products and service, so most of our money (or should I say overdraft) went on the 'front end'. I had a good suit, a decent laptop, up-to-date equipment for presenting and demonstrating, professional looking business cards and quality hand-outs. Our main office was a bedroom, with two business lines, but our business address was a smart, serviced office a couple of miles away. It worked. We created the illusion of being bigger than we were which brought us some great opportunities and of course, inevitably, one or two tricky moments that we were fortunately able to overcome using our initiative.

Example

A customer visiting from overseas insisted on coming to our 'offices' and meeting the staff. We did some quick thinking. We persuaded the serviced offices we used to let us put up our company sign in their own administrative area and the whole admin team agreed to act as part of our company, which really only employed two people, my wife and me.

The customer turned up, got shown around, met lots of people and then I took him straight out to lunch. Was he happy! He really thought we had a large team and very nice offices within the serviced office complex and continued to buy from us for many years. Of course, this only worked because we did in fact deliver a great product and quality service, but it illustrates the point that first impressions count.

Design your Logo and Strapline

Broadly speaking, design is about form and function: something has to look good and do a job. Good design is a way of communicating. If you have a well-designed company logo and strapline, it creates the right impression. To some extent, what constitutes good design is relative, but simplicity is the key, whatever the size or your organisation.

If, therefore you are a well-established company, check if your logo and strapline need a refresh, especially if it was designed prior to the internet revolution. If, on the other hand, you are a new operation then you have a blank page to work with, but for both, the design should fit the style and market you want to tap into.

Whatever kind of company you are, there are a couple of things you can do to get an idea of what other companies use to inspire you when you brief your local design agency or when you 'crowdsource' (I explain this later) the design. The best way of explaining this, is by working through an example and, for this purpose, we're going to imagine that we have a training company called Welearnmore.

The first thing we do is to go on Google, which has a great facility called 'Images'. Click on the Images button at the top left and type in your subject to view only pictures that are related to your search.

Our fictitious company, Welearnmore, is in the training arena. We Google 'training logo' under images, this will return over a million hits, but really we only need to look at the first dozen or so pages to get a choice of hundreds of different designs from all over the world.

In fact, even that is probably too many, so we will want to focus in on one, or maybe two, that will appeal particularly to the market we want to enter.

Now, the great thing with Google, is that if you hover with your mouse pointer over the image designs you like, a pop up box will say 'similar'. Click on the pop-up and you will see images similar to the one you like, from these, pick the one you like best, and you will get even more images, and then you keep going until you find an image that you like best. By going through this process, you will be able to find the one image on which you want to base your design, and you will have seen others that could influence your final logo design.

Crowdsourcing

Crowdsourcing is where a problem is sent out to a non-specific 'crowd' of unknown solvers, with a request or call for solutions from them. The web is a great place for crowdsourcing. People tend to be more open and less self-conscious in web-based projects as opposed to traditional ones for they feel they are not being judged or scrutinised. This ultimately allows for well-designed, artistic and original projects. A number of companies offer this service and it is an industry that is growing all the time. Google 'crowdsourcing design' and you will get a list of websites you can explore and as the projects are often open, you can see what the customer suggested and what the designers proposed. Prices and conditions do vary, so look at the T&Cs and some of the existing projects, before you decide.

Example

One of the companies we worked with was DesignCrowd. This is an online marketplace offering logo, website, print and graphic design services by providing access to freelance graphic designers and design studios around the world. According to its website, DesignCrowd has access to a 'virtual team' of 66,532 designers from around the world. We opted for an entry-level package, wrote a spec and published it on the website and quite quickly, we had a selection of designs on which we fed back about those we liked, and those we felt were not right. Eventually, we accepted one of the suggestions, got the designer to adjust some colours, and that became our new company logo. All for less than £200.

Consistent Branding

Your brand is you. So make sure you keep your branding consistent across everything you do. The logo should appear on every brochure, advert, web page, product – in fact, anything that has your name on. Seems self-evident, I know, but you will be surprised how many companies do not have a consistent approach to their outward-facing marketing and products.

Quality

Earlier I talked about image. One of its key elements, which I touch on later in the book, is quality, and how it affects people's perception of you. Make sure, therefore, that if you are going to use headed paper, you use good quality paper and that any graphics are clear and have bright colours. Please, never use inkjet based logos that smear when they get wet. First impressions are so important.

Logo Design Tips

As I have said before, keep it simple! Some of the best known brands in the world, like Nike and MacDonald's, are easily remembered, because they are simple.

Colours are important; I have always tried to keep the colours close to the product that we are selling and the industry we are in. Also, check what your logo looks like in greyscale, on business cards and on a mobile. It should be effective in every format and on every device. Our first logo didn't translate too well to a smaller format, so had to be redesigned, but luckily we spotted it early.

Keep fonts legible if you use text in your logo and keep it simple. Try not to get too carried away in trying to be trendy; what's fashionable today may date with time. Finally, make sure you get your logo designed using vector graphics, that way it is fully scalable from small to large.

Company Signage

Once you have a logo in place, it is a good idea to check how you are going to present it to the outside world if you have offices or retail premises. Be as big and bold as you can, and, again, ask the advice of the experts on where and how your details should be presented, remembering that your circumstances, customer and market, will influence your decision.

When we were involved with computers, I never really wanted to make much of a point about who we were, as we rarely had customers visit the offices, and as I didn't want it to be obvious that we had a lot of valuable equipment on the premises.

Many years later, when we had a different business, we opened up a new office with a training and conference room, and at that point signage became crucial. We wanted the potential client to feel we were a company worth dealing with, so big, bold and colourful, became the important requirement.

A quick tip for you here: it's worth doing what I call the 'walk-by test' with signage. If you run an operation that depends on passing traffic, such as a retail unit, ask yourself if you could be absolutely sure what you were selling if you were walking past and glanced in at the shop. If you are a café owner, ask yourself if people could see what you served. Remembering our principles of keeping it simple and focussed, you might solve this by highlighting what you specialise in, perhaps 'The Best Coffee and Brownies in Town,' for example.

Serviced Offices and Working from Home

Some of the best businesses have started from home. And when you first start out, I guess it is likely to be from home before progressing to external premises. Much depends on your business size and market, but in principle this is how most people develop. My wife and I started our main business from a bedroom with two desks and expanded into offices within the first year. At the time, there were fewer options for serviced offices, but this has changed significantly, and it is very likely that not far from you (unless you live in the wilds of Scotland) there is a serviced office you can use to help you create that all important first impression.

Perception is reality. If you're starting out and you want to give the impression of being a business larger than you are, you can take advantage of this human trait by creating the perception of a large business with the aid of serviced offices. If you're well established in your business, serviced offices are still useful, and we will talk later about how you can use them for expansion and how multiple locations can help you.

Some things apply to everyone. You need to have a proper mailing address – a PO Box address in the UK is not really taken that seriously, unless you are a major corporate - and you need to have a telephone that is answered professionally during normal business hours. Outside the UK, and certainly in places like the Middle East, a PO Box is standard, so it is seen as much more acceptable. I use Regus (www.regus.com), they have over 80 geographic locations in the UK and in big cities, there will be more than one; in London, for instance, there are around 50 offices alone.

Regus runs a number of packages, and one of the ones we started with was for a home-based business. With that you get a smart office address, a telephone answered in your name (calls can be transferred or messages taken), meeting rooms, you can rent ad-hoc, and the ability to use other Regus offices around the world. One of the benefits of using the same company for us was that we could negotiate in each country and the country that gave us the best deal, we would use to have a contract with; this mostly worked out better than a single contract in each location.

So, very quickly, and for a fixed fee, you can appear larger than you are and more professional. If you search for serviced offices in your area you will find a number of companies that offer the facility; with starting prices from around £60 per month (at the time of writing) from local companies, it is well worth doing. Add a picture of your new office on your website and newsletter, and you will also give out good signals to your prospects and customers and prove you are doing well.

One of the issues with selling outside your local area - and that could be in the UK or International - is creating the perception of a local presence. Every time we looked at a new country to develop business in, we would negotiate a deal for a serviced office, which gave us a local number and address and of course the facility to use meeting rooms if we required.

There is no doubt in my mind, that this helped us gain traction quicker than our competition, by giving the impression that we were local even though we initially never had anyone based there.

Localised brochures, web pages and business cards backed up the image. Once we had everything in place, then telephone enquiries would start to build up quite quickly.

With some offices, such as in South Africa, the time difference between there and the UK, meant we could get calls transferred when someone rang in. Sometimes, the person would cotton on that they were talking to someone in the UK, and ask why this was happening. We had a couple of revolving storylines that involved the local person being on holiday, at lunch or in a meeting, and that usually did the trick. In addition to South Africa, this worked particularly well in the USA, Middle East, Australia and New Zealand.

There are, of course, some trickier issues with time difference, and I have to say that it was more difficult than we had anticipated. We could go from one extreme on the west coast of America, to the other, in New Zealand; and I can't count the number of early mornings, late nights or weekends that the team spent bleary-eyed on the telephone, following-up messages to cover various parts of the world.

Operational challenges surfaced as well. When something didn't turn up in Dubai on a Sunday at 8 am and it was 4 am in the UK, it was difficult to resolve and a bit of a headache. But we learned from these incidents and allowed more time and found local people that could help ad-hoc with shipping and support. As things got busier, we would then recruit locally and build a team. As you can see, it's not simple, but you will get these challenges and like us, you will manage, adapt and change and find that it's a great journey that brings a lot of satisfaction as you watch the business flourish.

So, think about the next location you want to expand to, be it local or international, get some prices of serviced offices, and build a 'virtual' presence. Then be patient and resilient, and you will be surprised just how much local people want to deal with local offices - and all the hard work and effort will be worth it.

Example

We had a particular issue with the Middle East, where, with the different work days and hours, we were unable to always predict issues like packages being held at customs, or being delivered to the wrong address.

We asked around our contacts and found an English lady who worked part-time and had some great local knowledge. We agreed a rate, and for that small investment, we rarely had a package stuck or lost after that, and the customer was happy having someone they could contact locally. That local presence accelerated our business in the area, and eventually we needed, and found, the right country manager.

Martyn's Top Tips

- Keep it simple!
- Treat yourself and your business as part of the product or service you are selling.

- Make sure you look the part for what you are trying to convey.
- It's often what people perceive rather than what they know that influences their decisions.
- First impressions are very important and set the starting point.
- Remember your body language can influence what people think.
- Make sure designs translate to other formats and devices.
- Use serviced offices to promote your business brand.
- Use the crowd.
- Be consistent.

References and Resources

DesignCrowd: www.designcrowd.com.
Regus: www.regus.co.uk.

STEP 3

DRIVE BUSINESS TO YOUR WEBSITE

Step 3

"The best websites are better than reality."
~ Dr. Jakob Nielsen

A website or site is defined by Wikipedia as, "A set of related web pages containing content such as text, images, video and audio. A website is hosted on at least one web server, accessible via a network such as the internet or a private local area network through an Internet address known as a Uniform Resource Locator [URL]. All publicly accessible websites collectively constitute the World Wide Web."

This is so fundamentally important to the majority of business today, as most savvy buyers use either Google or YouTube to support their research into purchasing, that if you are selling services and products, then, as a minimum, you should have a website that at least allows your potential purchasers to find you and find out a bit more about you.

It still surprises me, therefore, that even now, given the huge influence the web has on all our lives, how many people still do not understand how important it is in their sales armoury. Many start-up businesses - and even established businesses - fail to maximise the opportunity the web presents to find potential customers and create that elusive mousetrap that will entice everyone to their door.

There could be many reasons, of course. One might be to do with the thought of the time required to sit down, think things through, write down the information and lay it out, before finding someone to create it. Another, might be the thought of the investment cost, which can tempt some organisations to put it together themselves, by using the many web design tools on the market.

However, considering the importance of the web in business, and that this is probably one of the most important investments you will make, next to the service or product you are selling, I would suggest that you can't afford not to spend time and money on getting a website and making it a good one that works! What do I mean?

Well, even a corner shop or bakery can benefit from a website. It can be used to advertise special offers, allow people to reserve orders, reach people out of the area, encourage people to sign up for emails, to keep abreast of new styles, and much more. Moreover, once your site is up, it needs to work. What do you do if the website doesn't load properly when people Google it? What if an enquiry form doesn't work? Imagine, then, the time it would take to fix it all and the business lost as frustrated customers click away. It was one of the big lessons I learned in business: spend money to save time, especially as it really doesn't have to be a lot.

I found my local web designer by searching local websites to see if I liked the design and looking at the bottom signature to see who built it. From this, I discovered Giles Butcher.

I supply him with the text and any photos and then, for a couple of hundred pounds or so, Giles will build me a perfectly laid out, basic website that looks good and works. For £500, he will build me a more complex site. Unless you are planning a very complex site with links to databases and the like, you shouldn't need to spend thousands of pounds.

I cannot emphasise enough how important it is to have a good, clear and simple website for your product or service, for once we have that in place, then we can start to build the areas that will raise your profile and bring you leads.

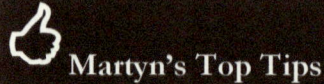

Martyn's Top Tips

- Give the website the attention it deserves.
- Keep designs simple.
- Spend money to save time.
- If you hope that your website will generate 80% of your business, then allocate at least 20% of your time to making it a great website.

References and Resources

Giles Butcher: www.netnous.co.uk

Content Marketing ~vs ~Search Engine Optimisation

Content marketing, as it is called, is the creation and publication of original content for the purpose of generating leads, enhancing your visibility and putting the company's subject-matter expertise on display. Content can mean blogs, case studies, White Papers, videos and photos.

In my time as an entrepreneur, and markedly so in the last couple of years, there has been a noticeable shift away from having the best-optimized websites, to having the website which provides the best content in and for one's key markets. Frankly, its importance cannot be overstated, simply because of the all-pervasiveness of the internet and the dramatic change in the way we use websites.

Some of the popularity of content marketing is its ability to generate qualified leads through engaging potential customers in a controlled environment at very little cost.

A recent survey in America summed it up very well. It showed that, 'content curation' (the latest buzz word), which was defined as the process of finding organizing and sharing content, "continues to gain strength as a top marketing strategy."

They also pointed out something for which you will have to find a solution, "Nearly 70 % of content curators say lack of time hinders their efforts, with 66 % saying a lack of original and quality content is a major drawback. Another 38 % say difficulty in measuring results is the stumbling block and 37 % say lack of staff to do the work is the hindrance." I do have an answer for this, and I cover it in more detail on the section on blogging.

Given the technological environment we live in, you may well have discovered that most of your potential customers are online, if this is the case, then the best strategy is to cover both bases, by having a well optimized website AND original content, which is what we are going to cover later in the book.

Brochure or Lead Generation Website

In my experience, and bear in mind you, the reader, may know a lot more than me about this technology, there are typically two main categories of websites: those that act as an online brochure and those that help generate leads. There are others that support manufacturers and service companies, but they are more to help existing customers than find new ones.

The Brochure Website

This is the kind of website that someone is only likely to visit because they want more information on the company, or want to confirm the type of organisation they are dealing with. It is unlikely that this category of website will show up in a general Google search, but will be on companies' headed paper and brochures, and will contain the usual headings of: 'About Us' 'Contact Us' 'Products' and, perhaps, some downloadable brochures.

It really is astonishing how many people and companies never really get much further than this. They probably see the website as a non-critical part of their business, and if that's the case for you, then that's great. I will make one observation, however: beware of being lazy and missing out a useful tool that could make you more successful.

The Business Driver Website

Bottom line, this is the website that will probably help with your - bottom line - so there are some basic things we need to get right before we can really make this kind of site work and as you may imagine they have a lot to do with the principles I discussed at the beginning of the book.

FIRST

Describe your Business or Product in Two or Three Words Maximum

Once again, we're going to use our fictitious training company called Welearnmore. We will say that it provides training and consultancy services across a wide range of subjects in the UK. Perhaps a good initial description would be, "The UK's Largest Training and Development Company."

Distilled from that would be 'training' & 'development' – but that's far too generic to work. Let's break it down further, by taking the strongest part of that - training - and look at the subjects that are taught. The most successful training courses are those aimed at project managers. That would now let us refine the words to 'project management' & 'training' – now we are starting to get somewhere (we could equally have refined the description according to geography like our earlier estate agent option giving us 'training and development Cheshire' which would also help us get listed quicker).

SECOND

Get the Domain and Email Name

Now we want to create a website that uses the key words as part of its web address or URL. Most words are available on domain names if you use multiple words separated by dashes. So, for example, www.projectmanagement-training.com is available. We register this address and will use it as our main lead generation programme.

You can register country specific domains, but, generally, I would go for the .com as the first choice, along with the local country such as .co.uk. You can use .org and .net and variations of the .com and co.uk names, but the preference is always a .com. Note that Google treats '-' as a space, so there is very little difference between 'mydomian.com' and 'my-domain.com'.

If you can get the name you want, and other country domains are available, then I would register them all, to stop a competitor using them at a later date. I would also check if your chosen domain name is available as a handle on all social media (I will cover this later) even if it is only to stop your competitors using it in the future.

Registering is easy and inexpensive. A typical domain name or web address is around £10 or less for a UK name, and whilst it varies more for a .net, .org or .com generally they are less than £20 and you can usually register for a number of years. Companies like www.ukreg.co.uk let you search on available names and suggest alternatives and will help you create email addresses, and, if required, provide hosting for your website. A web domain, five to 10 email addresses and web hosting space, should cost you less than £50 per year.

One other point to note: millions of people have been registering websites every year since the late nineties, all looking for the best combination of words so it won't surprise you to know that I have heard that there are no more three-letter domain names left, for example, so you may have to play around with words until you find what you want. Admittedly, you can purchase existing domain names, from companies such as sedo.com, but for most people creating the right combination of two or three words that reflect how customers will search for the product or service and what the business is and/or where it is, will be fine.

Example

I recently came across a small company based at its farm, called Farley Hall, that provided corporate days out and had set up everything under the web address farleyhall.co.uk or similar. As an online brochure to support sales activity, it was great. As a lead generation machine, it was a failure.

The company created a secondary website using the words corporatedayscheshire. The keywords captured how the customer would search and what the company did and where.

The business was soon coming out in the top five searches for anyone typing in: 'corporate days, Cheshire' or combinations of those keywords.

Search Engine Optimisation: An Easy Guide

Wikipedia describes search engine optimization (SEO) as, "The process of improving the visibility of a website or a web page in a search engine's 'natural' or un-paid ('organic' or 'algorithmic') search results. In general, the earlier (or higher ranked on the search results page) and more frequently a site appears in the search results list, the more visitors it will receive from the search engine's users. SEO may target different kinds of search, including image search, local search, video search, academic search, news search and industry-specific vertical search engines."

There are more companies than I care to count, who will sell you SEO or Search Engine Optimisation services with promises to get you in the top 10 on Google's first page. It is certainly a science; but follow a few simple rules in the design and upkeep of your website, and you will be able to get a top spot for your website without parting with a penny.

Please do not use Flash and Large Picture Animations

However nice it looks, put simply, Google will ignore Flash content, and this will impact your ranking. Large pictures and animations can take an age to load and the average user will click away from your site in seconds if there is a delay in loading. Keep to a good layout, simple colours and optimize any pictures for the web.

Use Page Title and Meta Descriptions

Sounds complex, but it is very simple and any web designer - or even you - can do it. . At the top of every web page is a description that helps Google understand your page and gives the description that will appear in your Google details.

To see for yourself, visit a competitor's website that has a good ranking on Google and use the menu (usually a right click on your mouse) to 'View' and 'View Source'.

You will get something like:

```
<!DOCTYPE html>
<head>
<title> Training &amp; XYZ Consultancy - Health and safety training, management, business coaching courses and project skills training</title>
<meta name="Keywords" content="general training, management training, courses, business coaching courses, training courses, management, interpersonal skills, team building, nvq, uk" />
<meta name="Description" content="XYZ Training and Consultancy: UK training and consultancy provider in the fields of health and safety training, project management, courses, personal skills, team building, leadership." />
```

<title> gives Google an idea of what your website is about. It will look at each of the words separated by commas.

<meta name="Keywords" content= helps Google to understand how to file your website away and the description will be what appears when your listing is online and searched on. So for our fictitious company, Welearnmore, using the website address www.projectmanagement-training.com to generate leads we could have the following:

```
<!DOCTYPE html>
<head>
<title> Welearnmore Project Management training and Consultancy - Project training, Project management, courses and project skills training</title>
<meta name="Keywords" content="Project management training and consultancy, project management, project training, courses, project team building, project coaching courses, training courses, consultancy, project skills, team building, nvq, uk" />
<meta name="Description" content="Welearnmore Project Management Training and Consultancy: The Leading UK training and consultancy provider for Project Management & Programme Management training courses, personal skills, team building and leadership." />
```

It really is that simple and it only remains to give you a couple of quick reminders. Remember to make the words match what you do so that Google knows what to do with your website. Throughout the process, ask yourself what your listing says about you. Remember not to fill up your keywords heading with too many keywords. Just create a quick message that makes the user want to click through to your website. This way when you get higher rankings, you'll get a better click-through rate!

Create Unique Title and Meta Tags for Each Page

This is a little more time consuming, you need to optimise every page the same way, but using a different description and different tags based on the content on the page. So once you have your main page right, repeat the exercise with your other pages as well. Google likes unique pages and we will talk a little later about using Google to help you with feedback.

Get Links to other High Ranking Sites

Google uses something called: 'PageRank' to help in its decision about how it positions you. Here's how Google describes it:
"PageRank reflects our view of the importance of web pages by considering more than 500 million variables and 2 billion terms. Pages that we believe are important pages receive a higher PageRank and are more likely to appear at the top of the search results."
In a nutshell, if a highly ranked site has a link to you, then you must be a trusted website, and the more links you have, the more trusted you become, and the more important you are.

Now, I hope you are still with me, as I am trying to keep this simple, at the same time as getting you to understand the importance of getting a grip on the basics.

If we go back to our fictitious company, Welearnmore, I would go to Google and search under our key words: 'project management training' and search in the country we operate in; for the UK we would search on Google.co.uk rather than Google.com.

The listings we would initially see, would be potential competitors, but as you work down the list, you will find agencies and consolidators that contain links for many companies. Some may be experts that offer links to approved companies, offer reviews from forums and offer recommendations from similar companies.
These are the companies you want to contact to see if you can set up a reciprocal link; some will charge and some will do it for free providing you link back. Try to keep away from really generic links that cover everyone and their dog, Google will see through that and discount it. The most important links are those to similar content websites.

Even if you only get a couple of links initially, persevere and keep looking and you will be surprised how quickly you can build up half a dozen links to relevant sites that rank reasonably high with Google.

In the past, I have also joined professional bodies in my area of expertise to get a listing on their web pages, so I can create a link to my listing from my own website. This is a powerful way of getting high value links.

Too Many Keywords can be Negative

It is hard to define what constitutes too many words, but if you aim to be brief that will help. Do remember to include the key words we set up in the meta tags within the body of the website. For our Welearnmore secondary website called www.projectmanagement-training.com, our text would be:

'Welearnmore Ltd. is one of the UK's largest providers of project management training and consultancy, helping build project teams and grow project skills.'

Gentle or subtle use of the phrase 'project management training' within the core text will help Google understand your key words to index on. If you overdo it, it is called 'keyword stuffing' which is pretty self-explanatory and which will earn you negative points!

Use of Alt Tags with Pictures and Images

An ALT tag is used in HTML and XHTML documents to specify alternative text (ALT text) that is to be shown when the element to which it is applied cannot be shown.

When you put a picture on your website, you can give the image an ALT attribute with an anchor. This is described with 'ALT', and if you look at the source code we described earlier, you can see the references to images, where it takes you if you click on it and the ALT details.

Let's say you have a picture of a training logo on your website, ask your web designer or edit the source and make sure you have an ALT tag that says something like alt='Welearnmore Project Management Training'.

Use the image (img) tag's ALT attribute and anchor (a) tag's TITLE attribute to your advantage. As with meta tags, don't stuff them with keywords. Use relevant keywords and key phrases which best describe the image. Properly using the ALT attribute can help you rank better in the image search results (Google image search) too.

Content Quantity and Quality

As mentioned earlier, Google will struggle to rank your website if you have only a few sentences of text, you need to have some reasonable content to make this work effectively. The magic number seems to be between 200 and 800 words, and try to keep it as unique as possible. As always, if you are unsure and all this sounds too technical, ask someone to help you. This is a really important part of the strategy to get right, so don't skip over it if it seems too technical!

Google Adwords

Adwords, also known as 'pay per click' or PPC advertising, is where you pay Google every time someone clicks on one of your adverts (more on that in a minute). How much you are willing to pay, dictates whether you appear at the top, middle or end of the advertising listings.

If you have ever searched on Google, you will often see the top three entries of the page are 'paid for' listings, the rest of the main section is made up of what are called organic listings and on the right hand side are the remainder of the paid for adverts.

Google Analytics: Capture and Keep Potential Customers

Once we have a well-designed website, optimised for the best web ranking results, the next task is to make sure that when potential customers land on our pages they stay with us and move through our other pages, rather than bouncing off elsewhere.

This is where Google Analytics comes in. There are thousands of articles written on Google Analytics, both on Google's pages and elsewhere, if you want to go into the subject in some detail. Google even gives free online training, but I think that by keeping it simple and focused, you will be able to do 80% of what you require without that, so I will only run through the basics.

Analytics is the number-crunching part of Google and will just about do anything with your data. It will slice and dice your website keywords and Adwords a hundred different ways, with a hundred different metrics telling you how your web pages are performing, so you can manage them. So, it won't just tell you how many people visit your website, but also how many stay and where they go to from your home page; in other words, the bounce rate. This is the number of visitors who enter the site and bounce off or leave without viewing another page divided by the number of website visits. If you get 100 visits a day and 20 of those visits do not visit any other part of the website, then you would have a bounce rate of 20% - which incidentally would be brilliant! There is no hard and fast rule, but Google Analytics specialist Avinash Kaushik reckons anything over 35% may be cause for concern and anything over 50% is worrying.

So how do we get people to stay? By their nature, people visit websites for information to help them for personal, career or other reasons. The key word here is 'information' and that's what we're going to look at next; for remember, we're thinking about the customer before anything else. There are several types of information that you can create for your customers to retain them.

Download Zone

A good website should have a download area that contains as much useful information as you can gather and keep up to date, all for free; I'll go into the reasons later. For example, on our www.projectmanagement-training.com website, we could have a download section that provides information for budding project managers. It could contain White Papers on why project management is important, case studies from customers showing how they implemented or used the service or product, sample templates such as project documentation, sample exam papers, if exams are part of training, and, of course, brochures.

Capture Potential Customers' Details

These documents should be factual and helpful, giving acknowledgements where they come from, other sources and providing your contact details at the end for customers to follow up, and, apart from the brochure, should not be blatant advertising and promotion. At this point you may be wondering what any of this has got to do with lead generation and driving business to your website.

Simple really! Once you have the documents in place and your friendly web designer has created a simple interface for people to click on and download, you then add a download form. This will ask people to provide their name, job title, company and phone number and it will ask, "Is there anything else we can help you with?" before they can access those valuable resources. At this point, the sceptics among you may say that you certainly wouldn't fill in a form, or that you would input rubbish text. Let me assure you from experience, that the majority of people will fill the form in correctly (especially if your downloads are good) and even if only one in three do, you will have more prospects than you had before.

This is a really valuable technique. By giving potential customers information that they desire or need, you capture information useful to your company, name, location etc. and numbers of people visiting.

Forums

In ancient Rome, the forum was a place of assembly. Several thousands of years later it has gone virtual. In fact, some might say that web forums were social media before the term was coined. They are certainly a good way to get people talking to you and to keep them on your site. It was one of the things that I set up fairly quickly to entice potential project manager trainees to leave questions that the team could answer, to present us as thought leaders providing information customers wanted.

Of course it was pretty blank at the beginning. So each day we would think up questions that we knew to be relevant to potential trainees and we would answer them; you could say it was a more like an in-depth FAQ (Frequently Asked Questions) list.

Well, that forum was picked up by Google and ranked. Soon we had potential project managers beating a path to our forum page asking questions and making comments to which we would reply the same or the next day. Over six months we became the most active forum in our specialist area helping to increase our download rates, improve our website ranking and helping to get the company noticed so that business came to our virtual door.

Think about how in your business you could try and anticipate what the most frequent questions would be and provide answers to get the ball rolling. A word of advice, though: if you start a forum on your website, do be aware of the investment required to keep it up-to-date, but remember, get it right, and it will drive potential customers to your website.

Decide if your website is a 'brochure' or sales tool.

- Describe your business or product in two or three words, maximum.
- Basic Search Engine Optimisation is easy – don't skip the basics!
- Google Adwords can help drive traffic - particularly whilst getting established.
- Google Analytics can give you the metrics to help you keep people on your site.
- Don't forget to 'capture' user information from visitors.
- Forums can be great to help towards your knowledge leadership.

References and Resources

Google Adwords Keyword Tool – A free tool to help you research words and phrases. https://adwords.Google.com/select/keywordtoolexternal

Wordtracker – has subscription based tools for researching and evaluating potential keywords and phrases. It will also help identify relevant websites to approach for linking to. www.wordtracker.com.

Google Adwords Training – Google has put some excellent training on the basics of using Adwords, well worth reading. http://support.Google.com/adwords/?hl=en.

Google has also put together a 30 page guide to Search Engine Optimisation and as it's by Google, it's a useful read. To find it, search Google for 'Search Engine Optimization Starter Guide' and you can download a .pdf version to read offline.

STEP 4

SOCIALISE SALES AND MARKETING WITH SOCIAL MEDIA

Step 4

"How can you squander even one more day not taking advantage of the greatest shifts of our generation? How dare you settle for less when the world has made it so easy for you to be remarkable?" ~ Seth Godin

Over the years, I have seen a remarkable change in the way that we as businesses find our potential customers. A huge driver in that change has been social media which has spawned social media marketing. Take a look at the background to its development and the social media statistics below, and you'll see the 'how' and the 'why' of this revolution.

Social media, according to Andreas M. Kaplan and Michael Haenlein, "… is a group of internet-based applications that build on the ideological and technological foundations of Web 2.0 and that allow the creation and exchange of User Generated Content." Or to put it another way, if you look at social media you will notice that people are in communities in which they talk, get involved and connect. Wikipedia says social media marketing "refers to the process of gaining website traffic or attention through social media sites". It also says that according to the European Journal of Social Psychology, one of the key components in successful social media marketing is building "social authority". This is developed when individuals or organisations establish themselves as "experts" in their given field, thereby becoming influencers in that field.

There you have it. Everything we are looking to do in this book, that is, quickly promote you, your service, product or company to be seen as an expert in your field, can all be done if we use social media well. Naturally, there are challenges, for it is very difficult to control social media, as the very freedom that it gives allows people to publicly feedback their views and experiences into the same market.

What you can do, nevertheless, is to begin participating in these electronic conversations with the expectation that you can influence the views of the audience.

'Conversation' is, in fact, a critical word to remember when you're socialising. For, one of the unspoken rules of social media is that no one likes direct or overt selling or marketing and those kinds of messages are on their way out. People are looking instead for industry experts and credibility. Once they feel that they can trust you and your information they will then be more likely to buy from you.

Social Statistics

- Social networking now accounts for 22% of all time spent online in the US.
- A total of 234 million people age 13 and older in the US used mobile devices in December 2009.

- Twitter has over 140 million active users and is thought to reach over 500 million accounts generating over 340 million tweets per day.
- Twitter has 10 million active users in the UK
- 80% of UK users access Twitter via mobile devices
- Australia has some of the highest social media usage in the world. In usage of Facebook Australia ranks highest, with over 9 million users spending almost 9 hours per month on the site.
- The number of social media users age 65 and older grew 100% throughout 2010, so that one in four people in that age group are now part of a social networking site.
- In June 2012, Facebook had 955 million monthly active users of which 81% were outside the US and Canada.
- It also had 552 million daily active users on average in June and 543 million active users who used Facebook mobile products in the same month.
- Facebook tops Google for weekly traffic in the US.
- iPod application downloads hit 1 billion in 9 months.
- If Facebook were a country, it would be the world's 3rd largest.
- Us Department of Education study revealed that online students out-performed those receiving face-to-face instruction.
- YouTube is the second largest search engine in the world.
- So there it is, social media is a reality for business today. Now it's time to learn what tools and techniques we need to make the most of it so we can an edge out the competition that is hopefully technically behind us or trying to over engineer a solution as most marketing departments do!

References and Resources

There is a good summary at 'seomoz' of all of the major social media websites, with a linked user guide on how to get the most out of them.

A good place to start for more detailed breakdown of demographics and positioning. http://www.seomoz.org/article/social-media-marketing-tactics.

Think Mobile: Think iPhone, iPad and Other Mobile Media

To make social media really work, you must have the right equipment and that means embracing the modern technology of smartphones and tablets. Why? Because people are increasingly working and communicating from their portable devices and you need to be able to interact with them in real time as the statistics below show very clearly.

Mobile statistics

- Mobile phones will overtake pcs as the most common web-access devices worldwide by 2013. It's estimated that the combined installed base of smartphones and browser-equipped enhanced phones will surpass 1.82 billion units by 2013, eclipsing the total of 1.78 billion pcs by then.
- More than 100 million people accessed Facebook solely from their mobile in June 2012.
- 18% of its over 500 million monthly mobile users don't visit the desktop site.
- Data indicates there will be nearly 6 billion mobile-cellular subscriptions by the end of 2011.
- There are twice as many mobile-broadband as fixed-broadband subscriptions.
- Strategy analytics predicts consumer and advertiser spend on mobile media will rise from just under $75 billion at the end of 2010 to just over $138.7 billion by 2015, at a 13.1% CAGR (includes handset browsing, applications, games, music, video, TV, ringtones, wallpapers, alerts and associated data).
- Gartner predicts that the location-based services user base will grow globally from 96 million in 2009 to more than 526 million in 2012.
- Facebook, Google Maps, Pandora and Weather Channel are the most popular apps across smartphones in us.
- Consumers downloaded some 2.4 billion mobile applications from app stores.

- Nearly 15 billion tickets will be delivered to subscribers mobile devices worldwide by 2014, compared to just over 2 billion this year.

I purchased the latest iPhone and iPad just so I could figure out how to use them in the business and what the mean to potential customers. I also watched how my children, part of the X-Box generation, used their smart devices so that I could make sure that as a company we used it to its full potential.

Example

We had a charity web page from which we would send out tweets on Twitter every time we picked up a new sponsor along with the prize details. Our followers then sold more raffle tickets which in turn brought on board more sponsors who saw how high a profile the event was getting.

There are many tools and apps available to help you use social media on the go; I won't cover them here, but just search for things like Tweetdeck, Hootsuite and Twitterfeed and find something that works for you.

Integrate your Social Media Marketing and Sales

Holistic selling is about making sure that your whole business is working together to increase sales and improve business so that you can keep the main thing, the main thing as I said at the start. An integrated plan is therefore a must-have element of that.

To create such a plan you need to think about what your business, sales and marketing objectives are and make sure that your social media supports all those activities. It also means that each social media message on each medium should complement the others.

We are therefore back to those keywords that we talked about at the beginning of the book when we were creating names for our website. If possible we want to have the same name for our website and for our social media medium names or handles but it's not essential as you will see with the names I come up with later on.

You can create a user name based on your primary website (which in our case would be Welearnmore), on your secondary website (which would be projectmanagment-training.com) or have an individual username. Having a company username rather than an individual one would ensure that the business was the focal point and not just you.

Martyn's Top Tips

- Devise a social media sales and marketing strategy that supports your business objectives.
- Think mobile
- Get a smartphone or tablet if you can afford one.
- Remember to focus on those key words.
- Watch how children learn and use mobile media – they are your future customers.

References and Resources

ITU: http://www.itu.int/ITU-D/ict/facts/2011/material/ICTFactsFigures2011.pdf.
ITU: http://www.itu.int/en/pages/default.aspx.
Facebook Statistics:
http://www.sec.gov/Archives/edgar/data/1326801/000119312512
325997/d371464d10q.htm.
Ofcom: http://media.ofcom.org.uk/facts/.

TWITTER

Twitter is something you love, loathe or are not sure about because you don't know where and how it fits in with everything that you do.

If we go back to its roots, we can see that in computing terms, Twitter has only been around a short while: Jack Dorsey created it in 2006 as a kind of SMS for the internet.

Commonly called social networking and microblogging, Twitter allows its users to read and send text-based posts of up to 140 characters, known as Tweets, to a global audience by computer, portable media and phone.

As of 2011, there are now 200 million users, generating over 200 million tweets and handling over 1.6 billion search queries per day.

Since its inception, Twitter has become many things to many people. Families might use it to stay in touch with each other. Groups use it to find like-minded organisations and people to join them.

Celebrities tweet the world about what they are up to at any given time. Businesses like ours can use it to co-ordinate activities, to market our products and services, to run events and so on.

I have never been one to follow famous people such as Stephen Fry, who has a huge following, but I do like to follow people that are in similar markets to me or who can supply information I need. What 'following' means in Twitter is that you will get a copy of any comments, observations or links for anyone you follow. Now while no one (except your loved ones) will ever want to know that you have just had a great cup of tea, people may want to hear your opinion or views if you are in their space.

In fact, Twitter is part of the whole approach to creating a profile for yourself, your company, product or services and, as we move through the various chapters, you will see how each of these areas is intertwined with the other. Twitter will play an important part in supporting what you do with other social media like LinkedIn and YouTube later on in the book.

Setting Up Twitter

Twitter is less about keywords, and more about creating a personal identity, where you are the expert. So let's start by creating a user for Twitter, although at this stage we are still being experimental, so this may not be your final username.

Go to www.twitter.com and if you are a first time user, you will be given a sign on screen to create your new identity. Enter the details as requested and create your username, you will need a valid email address. Going back to our fictitious company, we would create Welearnmore. Once created you will then get a choice of people to follow; the initial screen tends to be famous people, but let's go to the bottom and click 'interests'.

We can now type in our 'interest' in the top left search column. For Welearnmore we are going to use project management as our key, and straight away, we will get a list of the top Twitter accounts that also have those keywords in their profile. If you click on the paragraph for that Twitter account, on the right hand side, it will bring up a list of recent 'tweets' and the number of followers and the number of people that this tweeter also follows. Under project management, for example, you will see accrediting bodies such as PMI and APMG and also companies that sell products and services but that actually tweet general tips and information.

Using an example of a subject search of 'project management', you can see as an example the CEO of ProjectManager.com is giving out useful tips. We can see that he has written 656 tweets, has 4,596 followers and is following 1,311 people and at this point we can click on the 'follow' button. You can also click on the 'followers' link and that will show all the followers of the ProjectTips tweets. From this you can also 'follow' the 'followers' and, as a rule, generally, the followers of ProjectTips will be interested in the subject of Project Management.

What then happens is that the person you are 'following' gets notified that you are following them and he/she will often link back and follow you, particularly if they can see you are in the same space as them. You can then cherry pick your way down the list, follow anyone whose profile appeals to you and then continue down their chain. You will get an email every time you get a new follower, which is useful to keep track of your popularity.

But we mustn't get ahead of ourselves. We have got a while to go before we get to that stage, and need to get back to the basics of setting up our profile and sending some 'tweets' so anyone checking out our profile can see what 'tweets' we have done and if they are good will 'follow' us. Although it can take some months, you will be surprised how many people will find you and your followers will climb into the hundreds and hopefully the thousands. Don't forget that for people to follow you, you must be interesting, relevant, well informed and it also helps if you can be amusing as well!

The Strategy

First, we need to make sure our profile is up to date and here we will put important information about ourselves and what we do. You should also have a read through the other tabs, such as 'account', 'mobile' and 'applications', as you should put in as much detail as you can.

Upload a recent picture and fill in your bio to reflect our target market. Then we are ready to tweet our first tweet.

You will see the 'What's happening?' screen, for which you have 140 characters, to make your first observations. When someone searches for you or on a particular subject, the results are ranked for every user by name, username and the biography on your profile. To make sure you rank highly, make sure all your details are fully filled out and contain the key words that you want to be associated with your account.

Twitter has put together lots of guidance around creating and promoting yourself and your business, which you will find on their web pages, but in summary: share photos and videos, share event details and share behind-the-scenes information about your business, like projects under development. Users come to Twitter to get and share the latest, so give it to them!

The steps below will help.

- Regularly monitor the comments about your company, brand and products.
- Ask questions of your followers to glean valuable insights and show that you are listening.
- Respond to compliments and feedback in real time.
- Tweet updates about special offers, discounts and time-sensitive deals.
- Demonstrate wider leadership and know-how.
- Reference articles and links about the bigger picture as it relates to your business.
- Champion your stakeholders. Retweet and reply publicly to great tweets posted by your followers and customers.
- Establish the right voice. Twitter users tend to prefer a direct, genuine and of course, a likable tone from your business, but think about your voice as you Tweet. How do you want your business to appear to the Twitter community?

There are a couple of other things that you should be aware of and I've set them out below.

HashTags

Hashtags are a way of allowing users to search for certain strings, so, for example, if you search on #projectmanagement, you will see tweets that relate to the subject of project management. When you tweet in this subject area, you would add the term #projectmanagement to the end of the tweet. They have tried to create a central wiki for hashtags at www.hashtag.org but in the end they can be fairly random, so #projectmanagement could also be #projects, #PM, and so on.

Someone once explained this to me really well; if you search for #lost on twitter, you will find thousands of postings about the American show 'Lost', but you would not get posts on people that had 'lost' their wallet.

Have a search of similar tweets and see what hashtags your competitors use or just search on what you think is right and explore how many tweets there are containing those hashtags. I personally would not worry too much about hashtags until you become more proficient in using Twitter.

It's worth mentioning that there is another naming convention on Twitter as well, where you can have #projectmanagement or @projectmanagement, and they are dealt with in different ways.
Anything preceded with a '@' is seen as a reply towards a specific person or entity, much like 'To:' is in an email. So to reply to an entity called 'ProjectManagement', include @projectmanagement in the text, and it will appear as a 'mention' on their profile page.
Think along the lines of # being like 'about' or 'Re:' in an Email.

A good example of using '@' is exhibitions; most of them now have an @address which they use in the run-up to and during the event itself. The Learning and Technology 2013 show, for example, uses the tag, @LT13uk, anything tweeted using that name will appear directly in the organiser's 'mentions'.

When the exhibition takes place in January past, if you search on #LT13uk, you will see tweets from people that are at the show commenting on it, and you will also be able to give your own feedback.

One thing that has changed, as I complete writing this book, is that Twitter no longer automatically posts your tweets to your LinkedIn account; however updates on LinkedIn will appear on your twitter account when correctly configured.

URL Shortening

Because of the short number of characters you get in a tweet, trying to mention a web page link is almost impossible without using up all the text, so a bright spark invented URL shortening. In essence, short URLs allow a web address to be referred to in a tweet. For example, we recently ran a charity event and the web page link was: http://en-gb.Facebook.com/pages/Teddy-Bears-Picnic-at-Cholmondeley-Castle/175926085796153?sk=wall&filter=12

That was far too long for a tweet, so using a URL shortening service, I created a shorter link: http://bit.ly/r2noLP. How much easier is that? So my final tweet was:

'Come and visit us at the Teddy Bears Picnic on the 21st August - http://bit.ly/r2noLP'

There are many URL shortening services including Google and Twitter; however bear in mind that the short URL only works as long as the service you used to create the link continues to exist, so stick with the major players. I have registered with, and use, www.bit.ly, which allows you to see how many people clicked through your link. To try this service out go to www.bt.ly and register, to see how it works.

ReTweeting

One of the other popular and useful features is 'retweeting'. Sometimes you come across a tweet that you would like to share with your followers, the retweet (usually called RT) feature helps you and others quickly share the Tweet. At the same time if someone likes your tweet and retweets it, then it increases the spread of your message and improves your profile as a thought leader in your field.

Sharing Video

This is a great example of how all the social media threads come together and an indication of how each element of your business, sales and marketing plans are interrelated.

If we put up a short video on YouTube (discussed in more detail later), there will be a "share" icon which brings up Facebook, Twitter and Google Plus logos under the video to allow you to share it.

Click on the Twitter logo and it will open up a new window that takes you to your Twitter account, fill in a tweet for you about your video and then this will be posted to all your Twitter followers along with the URL and title. A similar process happens when you click on Facebook and Google Plus icons.

So now we are tweeting and sharing useful text as well as video information to engage and grow our followers. And you are starting to show yourself as an expert in your field, just by combining two aspects of social media and we haven't even started yet!

A word to the wise, bear in mind that once a 'tweet' or "retweet" is sent, it is instant, it cannot always be edited or deleted, only updated. To explain, Twitter says tweets can be deleted, but others say that even if you do delete it, it doesn't actually eliminate the tweet if it has already been picked up by search engines. Since Twitter can affect your image and your brand, I would err on the side of safety and assume that you can't delete.

Martyn's Top Tips

- Twitter is a great way to make you a knowledge authority in your market and to build your own community.
- Find out who your competition is connecting to.
- Use Hashtags to focus your tweets into particular areas.

- URL shortening can help you include a website address.

References and Resources

For a full list of features and facilities in Twitter, including setting up your profile, public and privacy settings and much more, got to the FAQ section of the www.twitter.com website.

Twitter produces its own guides for business which are good reading and provide some good tips to get you started.
https://business.Twitter.com/en/basics/what-is-Twitter/
Repository of hashtags: www.hashtag.org.
Teddy Bears Picnic: http://www.teddybears-picnic.co.uk/
ProjectManager.com @ProjectTips.
Learning Technologies 2013:
http://www.learningtechnologies.co.uk/

BLOGS

A blog, short for web log, is a website which can serve a multitude of purposes. A blog can be a diary, a medium for exchanging information, a soapbox to air views, or a place to pass on news; in fact, it can really be about anything you want to write about on an on-going basis to connect with people and keep your subscribers up to date with the latest information. They in turn can connect back to you by leaving comments, by linking to you and by emailing you. A blogger is someone that blogs and the blogosphere is just a generic term for referring to blogs generally.

There are two types of blogs: personal and business. The personal blog is a place to share everyday happenings, thoughts and personal photos; it's a cross between a virtual, interactive diary and letter to friends and family.

Example

When we built our house, we had a lot of family enquiring about how it was going and where we were up to on a regular basis. So I set up a blog to which I uploaded pictures and passed on what was happening at any stage and family and friends would respond by adding their comments and views allowing for some lively debate on some of the techniques used as you can be sure.

At the end of a year the blog had built up to quite a substantial online diary. So when we had finished I used a tool called blog2print and they turned the whole blog into a really nice hardcover book, which now features on the coffee table.

A business blog follows a similar pattern, but we are now creating stories about the company or product, press releases, news, updates, research, stories, personal comments from designers, coders and just general interesting facts. Your business blog will allow you to communicate information to potential customers and to interact with them through content marketing or 'content curation', the latest buzz word.

The blog is, in fact, one of your holistic sales and marketing tools. For whereas your website will have valuable but fairly static information, your blog will be a dynamic, updateable, detailed and personalised diary which you can use to reach and influence your market.

Twitter's blog is a great example of what I mean with its regular updates of news, views and changes which it then tweets about as you can. It's not the only influential blog out there. There are others ranging from online newspaper-type blogs, to technical blogs, to self-styled opinion blogs.

In my marketplace there are a couple of blogs that are very vocal about standards and direction. Possibly as a result of this, they attract a huge and active user base, whose conversations find their way into search engines, which make manufacturers and service providers vie with each other to get their products mentioned and get good reviews.

Setting up a Blog

There are many providers of blogging tools, but for this lesson I am going to stick to www.blogger.com, which is part of Google to give you a basic handle on how to approach the process.

On the blogger page you will see "Create a Blog" in an orange box. You will need an account with Google, so if you have one in place, sign in, otherwise follow the instructions to create your new account.
Once you have your account, then you are ready to start your blog. You will see a couple of boxes on the screen as in the example below. The title should reflect the subject and contain one or two of the keywords that we have discussed in previous chapters.

The second part is a slightly trickier in that you now have to find a unique name for your blog which will become http://www.yourname.blogspot.com . Bearing in mind there are millions of blogs, you may have to be flexible in how you name it, but again try and keep your keywords within the title. Finally, choose a design that you like and you are ready to go. You do have the option of changing the design template and layout later on, so don't worry too much about it at this stage. Once you have found a unique name, Google will take you to the Blogspot Dashboard for your account and you can start blogging.

From this point on, there are lots of things you can do with your blog. To get ideas, Google 'top 10 blogs' for a look at professionals at work, then search under your competitors' company name and add 'blog' to the search term. This will show you if they have a blog or blogs and you can see what they say and how often they say it.

The key point to remember that it's not about innovating; it's about taking a good idea and improving it. So look for the things that your competitors do in their blogs and see where you would change it. Look at how they link to people, what tools they use, who subscribes to them, how they handle comments and how often they post.

Once you get the hang of posting information, you need to start promoting your blog to get on the radar of the people you want to be your customers. As we are using our blog as part of the wider promotion of our company, product and services, there are some things that you need to account for.

Blogs and Search Engines

To make sure your blog is visible to the outside world there are settings that need to be done. The options for these are on the 'Settings' page, go to 'Basic', and then 'edit' to change the settings. Here's what you will see.

- **'Let search engines find your blog?'** setting determines whether or not your blog will be included in Google Blog Search and if it will send a signal to Weblogs.com, a service which continually displays recently updated blogs, letting them know that you've made a new post. If you select "No," everyone can still view your blog but search engines will be instructed not to include it in their listings.

- **'Install email this post.'** Use this on your blog and people will be able to forward your posts to friends. This may not have an immediate impact on your site stats but it enables others to publicise your blog for you.
- **'Turn on post pages.'** By publishing every post as its very own web page, you ensure that your entries are way more link-able and more attractive to search engines. This is very important if you are blogging your business.
- **'Turn on your site feed.'** When people subscribe to your site feed with their newsreaders, they're very likely going to read your post.
- **'Add your blog to blogger's listings.'** When you add your blog to the listings it shows up in "Nextblog", "Recently Updated" and other places. It's like opting-in to traffic.

Essential Blogging Tips

Blogging is simple but there are some essential tips that will maximise your effort and minimise the hassle.

- **Write quality content and do it well.** If your 'style' is bad writing, worse grammar, no punctuation, that might be okay for a niche crowd but it's not good enough if you're going achieve mass appeal, so make it look professional.
- **Publish regular updates.** Simple really, the more you blog, the more traffic you'll get.
- **Think of your audience.** Speak to one person in particular. When you keep your audience in mind, your writing gains focus. Focus goes a long way towards repeat visitors.
- **Keep search engines in mind.** There are a few things you can do to make your blog more search engine friendly. Use post titles and post page archiving. This will automatically give each of your post pages an intelligent name based on the title of your post. Also, try to be descriptive when you blog. A well-crafted post about something very specific can end up very near the top results of a search. Remember to categorise your blogs into topic areas so that people can see the kinds of things you post

about and so that they can find posts they might be interested in.

- **Keep your posts and paragraphs short.** Strive for succinct posts that put pertinent new information into the blogosphere and move on. Keep it short and sweet so visitors can pop in, read up and click on.
- **Put your blog URL in your email signature.** Think of how many forwarded emails you've seen in your day and just imagine the possibilities.
- **Submit your address to blog search sites and directories.** People look for blog content at Technorati every day, are you on their list? You should be. Submit your blog's web address to Technorati, Daypop, Blogdex, Popdex, Articlesbase and any other site of that kind you come across. Use Google to find the web address, then each site has simple instructions on how to submit your address.
- **Link to other blogs.** Links are really important in the blogosphere and it takes information to make information so start linking to relevant blogs in your area.
- **Be an active commenter.** This is in the same vein as linking. Most comment systems on other blogs and forums also provide a way for you to leave a link back to your blog, which invites a visit at the very least. So if you feel inspired, leave a well-thought out comment in your blog travels.
- **Enable following on your blog.** Following is a great way to keep your customers updated on the latest activity on your blog. New blogs will have this blog feature enabled by default, but for older blogs you will have to enable it from the 'Layout' and 'Page Elements' tab.

It is really important to realise that you are only as good as the information you post and an initial fizz of writing skills can easily slip away as other things become more important. So how do you stop this happening? The answer is good content and I go into this in the next section.

- The difficult bit with blogging is keeping the content and comments flowing, so make sure you do.
- Don't forget search engines like Google will index your blog entries.
- Put your blog URL in your email signature so everyone sees it.

References and Resources

Blogger: www.blogger.com.
Our friends at Google do a good guide to blogging – if you search for 'Google Blogging Guide' you will get a comprehensive guide including videos on setting up a blog from scratch.
WordPress is another popular way to blog: www.wordpress.com.
Technorati: www.technorati.com.
Popdex: www.popdex.org.
Articlesbase: www.articlesbase.com.

YOUTUBE

I am sure at some time or other you have watched a video clip or two on YouTube from funny clips like 'Charlie Bit My Finger', to sports highlights, to national events and educational clips. As YouTube statistics show, it has a huge influence, certainly amongst the younger generation, but increasingly across the ages.

YouTube Statistics

- The second largest search engine in the world.
- The third most visited website in the world.
- The world's largest video sharing platform.
- Over 800 million unique users visit YouTube.
- Over 4 billion hours of video are watched.
- 72 hours of video are uploaded to YouTube every minute.
- 70% of YouTube traffic comes from outside the US.
- YouTube is localised in 43 countries and across 60 languages.
- In 2011, YouTube had more than 1 trillion views or around 140 views for every person on earth.
- In one minute online there are 2.8 million videos viewed.
- YouTube is available over 350 million mobile devices.

As a result the second largest search engine in the world should form part of your strategy in developing your business further.

Example

Take the time I wanted to learn to play the guitar. Rather than have a tutor or go to classes I wanted to learn from a website. To find my ideal website, I could have used engines like Google. I chose YouTube instead, typed in my search words and thousands of results came up. So far, so good.

But now we come to the difference. On Google, I would have had to go through each page, click through to each link and then make my own judgment. On YouTube each video clip came with information on the number of times it had been viewed and useful comments from others who had tried the video lessons. (This is a good lesson about YouTube, for given limited time, this is the sort of information people will use to decide which video to watch and work back from that point.)

When I started my 'free' guitar lessons online at the end of each clip was the web address of the company that filmed them and when you clicked to their website, there were offers for further tutorial material. Because I liked the YouTube clips, I purchased a DVD and supporting book from them.

YouTube was good for the company and good for me. I was happy because I purchased from someone that had proved to me they had a track record because of the samples I saw and the comments I read. They were happy because by giving something away for free they got a customer who spent some money. Everyone was a winner.

Hopefully you can now see how YouTube can support the next part of the holistic selling model, where we use the search engine to support and give confidence to the potential buyer of your services.

How to Post Video's on YouTube

First do the research. Learn from competitors and follow a product or service you understand. Note how it is presented, the quality of the clips, the feedback and comments and look at the number of views.

Some companies set up their own channel, so you can click on the web link, usually on their main website and it will take you to YouTube, automatically listing all the video clips associated with that company. Once you have seen a few clips, an idea should be forming in your mind on how you can do something similar or even better for your business and then you can get down to work.

Go on to YouTube and create an account, in your own name if you want to experiment for a bit before going live, or in your company, product or marketplace name, if you plan on starting straight away.

Once again we are back to our common theme of keeping keywords consistent, so an ideal username would contain the keywords discussed earlier.

For example, if I were setting up an account for Welearnmore, I would probably try and create a user called Projectman or projecttraining. Don't forget, you can add numbers so we could equally be Projectman123.

Where to Start

In our 'YouTube generation' it's worth pointing out there are lots of people trying to get a reputation for creating videos and because of that, someone you know or a friend of a friend, may be able to help you create, edit and distribute the type of clips we are going to discuss below. If you can find someone (film school students might be willing to try their hand at this), and agree a nominal rate, then it will save you time, otherwise you can go the DIY route, as I first did and create your own.

I have used a webcam, a video camera and all sorts of technology to try and get clips I liked. My early clips looked OK, but the sound echoed. Once I fixed the sound, I realised the quality needed to get better and on the changes went as I came to understand the medium and my aims better.

The point is, it doesn't have to be perfect from day one, it can cost quite a lot of money to get the proper equipment together and starting with something is better than not starting at all.

Actually, most modern webcams have a pretty good resolution and are OK for filming but sound is always an issue. The first thing we invested in was a decent microphone, a wired one that plugged into the laptop and clipped on the lapel of the subject expert, and that made a big difference straight away.

Then came the question of editing the clips, and matching the audio up, for which we used one of the many free and basic editors on the market. We used Adobe Premier, which was a reasonable price, but if you have a Mac then the iMovie software is excellent. Then we wrapped in some titles and links at the end to hopefully get the customer back to our website.

Eventually, you will want more but actually a good high quality, video costs less than £200 and if you use a memory card or stick you can generally just plug it straight into the laptop. Once we got more confident, we used a video recorder, wireless microphone, a portable backdrop (blue) and some free autocue software running on the laptop to help prompt the subject matter expert.
We also invested in a couple of movie style lights to help give better consistent lighting, and, for under a £100, they proved a good investment.

We also found it easier to use an actor rather than our subject matter expert. Strange as it may seem, the subject matter expert was great in a classroom, but came across a bit 'wooden' in the video. The actor, whilst knowing absolutely nothing about our products and markets, could use briefing notes and an autocue and come across as far more credible in a single take. The best thing was that our actor cost us less than the day rate of the subject matter expert, who could be out earning money; it also helped that he had a studio we could use for filming.

The reason for the blue backdrop (blue screen) was that we could use something called Chroma Key, where most good video editing software can replace the blue background with anything we wanted, much like most modern TV and films. Once we had this then we could create animations on a computer and overlay them onto the video, so our subject matter expert would be standing on the left of the screen whilst animations appeared to his right. It all sounds very complicated, but you have to bear in mind it took us a couple of years to get to this maturity level, so start with what you have and develop it from there.

The Subject

Like my guitar playing example, think about your niche and the keywords that describe your business. In our Welearnmore example, we are project management experts, so short videos on subjects such as: top ten project management tips, how to maintain quality, project budgets and project management, scope creep and how to control it, are just a few examples of topics for this particular market.

I assume at some stage someone will have a problem with budgets in their project, so my video on "project budgets" and "project management," will hopefully be picked up by someone searching YouTube. The introduction will say a few words about my company and at the end of the clip we will give our Twitter, blog and website addresses, with the offer of free downloads on the website for further supporting material.

Now, if you have this right, and a prospect likes your YouTube video, they are likely to subscribe to your Twitter account and blog. They will then visit your website (with the Twitter and blog links 'subscribe' button available to click on) to download the free supporting documents and as part of having access to your website downloads area, they have to register their details.

As I mentioned before, not everyone will register, but the majority will and you have your first leads coming through to you. Mention the YouTube video on your Twitter account (to which you have the option of linking when you set up) so all your followers see the link can retweet it if they like it, which can in turn be retweeted by their followers and on it goes.

In your blog you should refer to the video, with perhaps a more detailed explanation of what the video is about and the benefits. Your blog followers can leave comments on it and forward through the email facility a copy of the link to their friends.

If you get the groundwork right you can see how this can develop into a circle of information that hopefully raises your visibility as an 'expert' in your particular field. It will not happen overnight, but keep making the video clips, keep blogging and sending those tweets and it won't be long before you are that bit smarter than most people in your marketplace and the Zulu Principle starts.

Google will pick up the information from all these sources and this will start the process of you being recognized as a subject matter expert, a thought leader and getting your sites ranked higher. The more you update your social media, the higher and faster rankings you will get on Google.

Your common keywords will appear in everything you do and when you type those keywords into Google you will be surprised how much of an industry leader you will look.

It is hard work keeping all this flowing, but before long, potential prospects will come to you when they want something in your area, as you will have created the perception of being an expert in your field.

YouTube for Business

YouTube has created a concept called 'Brand Channels' which allows a company to create a more bespoke interface, so that potential customers have a custom landing area, with more of the look and feel of their company. When the customer lands in your area, a video can be played automatically and other relevant videos are listed as well and again they all play within the branded window.

If you want to a channel that is aimed at just your products, this may be the way to go; a good example is the 'Royal Channel' which is the official channel of the British Monarchy. Just search YouTube for Royal Channel and you can see how they have branded it to look very 'Royal' – and of course with over 38 million views, it clearly works for them!

The brand channel service tends to be a bit more bespoke and if you search 'channels' on YouTube it will give you more information on the process involved.

Martyn's Top Tips

- Use the search engine to support and give confidence to the potential buyer of your services

References and Resources

Adobe Premier: http://www.adobe.com/products/premiere.html
iMovie: http://www.apple.com/uk/apps/imovie/?cid=mc-features-uk-g-fea-imo-imovie
Brand channels:
http://www.youtube.com/t/advertising_brand_channels.
The Royal Channel:
http://www.youtube.com/user/theroyalchannel?feature=results_main.
YouTube: Video Revolution 2.0 (YouTube Statistics 2012).

FACEBOOK

This is how Wikipedia describes this phenomenon: "Facebook is a social networking service that lets you connect with friends, co-workers and others who share similar interests or who have common backgrounds. Many use it as a way to stay in touch after finishing school or as a way to share their life publicly. What makes Facebook different from other social networks, is its extensive privacy controls, its development platform and its large and quickly growing user base. Facebook has been called the "thinking person's" social network. Compared to many other social networks, Facebook gets new features and improvements on a regular basis."

Like many people I have always seen Facebook as pretty much a personal thing; my family and friends use it to post and update each other and for that purpose it works a treat. Now however, a huge number of businesses have Fan pages and consolidate these with links in TV and magazine adverts that try to get people like you and me to follow them on Facebook.

This shift has happened particularly over the last couple of years and I thought it worth looking at how Facebook can work for business and how it can be used in your marketing and raising awareness programmes.

The Strategy

The first thing is to ask yourself some questions. What is your strategy? What do you have that is unique either within your brand or story? Who are your potential customers? How will you connect with them? What bits of what you do, do you think will be important to them? What are your goals?

Another good question to ask is why do you want to be on Facebook? Are you creating a knowledge area, better customer service or do you want your page to drive sales or traffic? In a retail environment for example you may want to drive customers to visit your location or in a business-to-consumer company perhaps you want to sell off the page.

Setting up a Business Page

Facebook makes it really easy to set up a business page. Its 'Best Practice Guide to Marketing on Facebook' gives a lot of detail and background on how to start and make it work for you and 'Building Your Business with Facebook Pages' gives you everything you need to know, complete with detailed examples to show you how Facebook may be able to work for you. Understanding the capabilities of Facebook will help you develop a good long term strategy for not only creating your pages but ensuring you build a successful community on this social media platform. Once you know what you're going to do with Facebook you need to set up a fan page and you will be given a number of choices.

Once you have chosen the option you think will work best, it will take you through some additional information about the category of your business and finally confirmation of your email address, if you are not already a user. You now have a Facebook page for your business.

Example

A local Italian café has been using Facebook successfully to promote itself and its range of home-made food. They have small, laminated cards on the tables with their Facebook details and a competition with prize every month for the best uploaded photo of a meal or food taken at the café.

The café also post videos on YouTube of how they create dishes such as their pizzas and videos telling customers how they can make good cappuccino and espresso coffee. They also comment back on any Facebook posts and keep up a good natured banter with everyone. These simple steps have built a regular and growing community of loyal and local contributors and customers.

I have a couple of final tips for you. Allow wall posts so that customers can express how they feel and so you encourage customer interaction. Allow photos to be uploaded so that people can 'tag' themselves using your product; people love pictures. Think too about if you want a one-stop-shop as you can add a 'product' tab that allows people to view your products and purchase them, without leaving the website.

All this may seem overwhelming, and at first you may well be unsure how to determine which features to use, but it's easier than you think. As time goes on you will find that you grow into it through understanding your business and customers better, and through keeping things simple and focused in on what you do best.

References and Resources

Facebook www.facebook.com
Building Your Business with Facebook Pages
Facebook Ads Page Optimization Guide
http://ads.ak.Facebook.com/ads/FacebookAds/PagesOptimizatio nGuide_082211.pdf.
Best Practice Guide – Marketing on Facebook
http://ads.ak.Facebook.com/ads/FacebookAds/Best_Practice_Gui de_042811_10.pdf.
Facebook Insights - Product Guide for Facebook Page owners
http://ads.ak.Facebook.com/ads/FacebookAds/Pages_Insights_G uide_Updated.pdf

LINKEDIN

Technically, LinkedIn is a global professional networking tool. Actually, it's a whole lot more and that's why it's useful for business. A bit of back-story first.

I joined LinkedIn when it was in its early days, I think somewhere around 750,000th member, which sounds high, until you consider that LinkedIn now has over 120 million members across 200 countries and is probably the largest business networking website worldwide. According to Wikipedia, LinkedIn membership grows by a new member approximately every second. About half of the members are in the United States and 11 million are from Europe. With 3 million members, India has the fastest-growing network of users as of 2009. The Netherlands has the highest adoption rate per capita outside the US at 30%. LinkedIn recently reached 4 million users in UK, 1 million in Spain and nearly 1 million in Pakistan.

What the world has discovered is that LinkedIn is a great tool for personal and business use. I tend to use it as a reference for things I want to get into or for finding contacts and, of course, for making sure that people find me and that my profile and my activities say exactly what I want them to say. I make sure that my profile is up-to-date and that I have some good recommendations from colleagues and customers. I also share my PowerPoint slides, my reading list and link in my Twitter account and check in regularly via my smartphone so that I can update, search and post on the go.

Business Use of Networking

There is so much you can now do with LinkedIn beyond basic networking. Increase your visibility as a company and as an individual by creating or joining groups of like-minded people. Search and connect with people either in the industry you are in or more importantly the industry, area or country that you would like to be in. Improve your Google page rank and optimise your blog or website searchability by using features on LinkedIn that are for that purpose. Check out the reputation of potential customers and at the same time the competition. Recruit the right people for your vacancies; recently we created a 'pay-per-click' ad looking for a sales manager based out of Poland, and very quickly we had over sixty people send in their details.

Setting Up

Setting up a LinkedIn account is very simple. Google 'LinkedIn' and register, then work your way through the setting-up process filling in details of your employment history and current position. It's a chance to make a subtle sales pitch about what you are now doing.

Don't forget to include your keywords where possible as Google will pick up and index your LinkedIn profile. You'll be given the option of signing up for free registration or a premium service; for what we want to achieve, the free service more than covers our requirements.

Once you set up the account, you will have a number of options to customize your profile, including linking your Twitter account, creating a SlideShare account (more information on that can be found further on) and setting up your recommended 'reading list'.

When a potential customer or company does a search on you ensure they see what you want them to see. So make sure you review the information and keep it up to date as your business changes and grows.

Groups

Once you have your profile in place then you can join any of the tens of thousands 'groups' covering every subject you can think of, but like Pareto's 80/20 rule, only around 20% of them have a large membership base, and they are the ones you want to join initially.

First, find the subjects you are interested in, and you may see that there may be a group in each country for that subject or one single global group. Some groups are membership only, so you will apply to join and the moderator of that group will decide whether to accept you application. They may accept you immediately or they may ask why you want to join the group so make sure that you know. Once you are in the group you will then have access to its members and you can see their details.

If we were promoting Welearnmore, we would search for groups on project management and look at the details of each group and its membership numbers. No point in joining a group unless it has an active and large user base. From there, you can look at the membership base and issue an invitation to selected members to connect with you. LinkedIn requires you to have some 'link' to the person you invite which is fine since we are in the same group. The person you invite to connect is likely to review your profile and hopefully will accept your invitation.

Day-to-Day Use of LinkedIn

From a personal perspective, I am happy to link out to around 200 people, some people on LinkedIn will connect with 500+ contacts, I guess it depends on what your business is – if you were in recruiting for example - then bigger numbers would be better.

People and Organisations

When I want to break into a company, I search for the company and then select the type of people I wanted to connect with. This is a good search to use both nationally and internationally.

Example

When I was looking to break into a new telecoms company in the Middle East, I used LinkedIn to find employees of this company then concentrated on finding the project managers and IT people.

Once I had found the right people, I then sent out a request to connect and most of the time they would accept and connect back to me.

Once I had connected to a couple of key people, I then had access to their email, sometimes personal or through LinkedIn, which allowed me to introduce myself. This strategy has worked really well for me and has been instrumental in opening up accounts overseas.

You will notice on your home page that LinkedIn will suggest people to connect to. Based on its profile of your contacts so far, it will show any updates from your connections and if you have linked in to Twitter, it will show your latest tweets. It's worth pointing out that when you tweet, it will appear in your status update to your connections, so bear in mind that everything you say will appear connected to everyone. There is so much more you can use LinkedIn for, but I wanted to cover the basics so that we continue to create the circle of information that is holistic selling. For a complete picture, it's worth taking a full tour and seeing if the premium services would work for your business.

Once you have got started with LinkedIn, you will see that in a short time you have an online profile which will appear in Google, you have joined groups of interest to you and hopefully you have some networked contacts that have accepted your request to link.

Treat LinkedIn rather like Twitter; post regular updates on the 'what am I doing now' box and join in and post on your selected groups, perhaps joining an existing discussion or as you get more confident, starting your own discussions and even your own group. As your contributions build up, it will add credibility to your reputation, business, services and products, building confidence in the people you want to become your customers in the future.

👍 Martyn's Top Tips

- Join groups.
- Use it for researching individuals and companies.
- Treat LinkedIn Like Twitter.

References and Resources

LinkedIn: http://uk.linkedin.com/

SLIDESHARE

Although SlideShare.net is a relatively new service launched in 2006, the website gets an estimated 58 million unique visitors a month, and has about 16 million registered users who use what you might call, YouTube for slides.

People put up a slideshow for everyone to see and they can allow other users to download it or just view it. There are thousands of slide shows on pretty much every subject you can think of, and I upload the main slides I use in my presentations and save them using the same keywords I have everywhere else.

If someone is searching for slides, perhaps to do an internal presentation to their business, or just to get further information for research purposes, then it seems reasonable to let them have access to my information, statistics and general data. The fact that they use my slides with my visible contact details, will add some credibility to my company or myself at some stage in the future.

It also means my details are coming up when people search for slides on that subject. So the same potential customer may have Googled my specialist keywords, found my slides, seen my blog posts, read my tweets, seen a YouTube video explaining it and started to think that I was an expert in my field and, as a result, they would come and talk to me when they wanted to progress further.

It is very simple to register and upload slideshows and you will be amazed at just how good some of the presentations are, take some time to look at a few, particularly the one on 'Death by PowerPoint' and the ones on social media. There are some really good ideas that you may be able to use in your own presentations to give you the edge that you need in business.

References and Resources

SlideShare: http://www.slideshare.net/

Death by PowerPoint:
http://www.slideshare.net/thecroaker/death-by-powerpoint

PINTEREST

At the time of writing there is a new social media kid on the block called Pinterest. Even in the short time it has been around it seems to have done very well: in December 2011 it came from nowhere to the top five slot in Hitwise's list of the top 10 social networks.

The concept is simple. Users of Pinterest curate themed image boards, populating them with media found online using the "Pin It" button or uploaded from their computer. Each such item of media is known as a "pin" and can be a picture, a video, a discussion or a monetary gift. Pins can be grouped into "boards", which are sets of pins created on a given topic. Pinterest can be accessed by adding the "pin it" button to the desktop bookmark bar, the "follow me" and "pin it" buttons added to a personal website or blog pages, and the Pinterest iPhone application available through the App Store.

Joining

You need to register on the Pinterest website (www.pinterest.com) for an invitation to join, and then spend some time looking at the most popular pinboards, to see why they are working so well.

Business

Pinterest are quoted as saying, "Pinterest lets you organise and share all the beautiful things you find on the web. People use pinboards to plan their weddings, decorate their homes and organise their favorite recipes. Best of all, you can browse pin boards created by other people. Browsing pin boards is a fun way to discover new things and get inspiration from people who share your interests."

Not what might you call an obvious social medium for businesses but Pinterest has been driving more referrals and traffic than many existing social networks. Businesses use Pinterest to advertise special offers, promote products and services and pass on information in order to draw people to their website or shop or outlet.

Blogger Kate Bryan started using Pinterest to 'pin' her work and has since had over 10 million page views and attracted more than 16000 blog subscribers. She is quoted as saying that her top 10 traffic sources are from Pinterest.

My wife used Pinterest to browse shoes, pictures of which were put up by people that owned them or had spotted them; the range and diversity was quite amazing and useful. Within a few clicks you can be at the manufacturer's website to place an order.

Within our business, I plan to take screenshots of some of our white papers and books and add them to a relevant board as part of establishing myself in thought leadership as we have previously discussed. Within this, I will, where possible, include links back to my website and landing pages, and hopefully this in turn will drive more traffic.

These kinds of experiences make Pinterest worth investigating as do its strong links with Twitter, Facebook, YouTube and Google Plus as they increase the ties between social media and contribute to making ourselves smarter and gaining that all important edge.

For while Twitter, Facebook and Google Plus combine words, pictures and video, and Youtube defines the 'video' generation, Pinterest is about pictures in a more structured way than anyone else to date.

Nevertheless, it's too early to let you know how I think I will do, and if Pinterest will become a major force in the long term, but early adoption of any of these technologies allows you to claim key words early on and if it works, then you have the edge.

References and Resources

Hitwise – www.hitwise.com
Kate Bryan: http://www.thesmallthingsblog.com/.
Pinterest: http://pinterest.com/.

GOOGLE+

Wikipedia describes Google+ (pronounced and written as Google Plus or as G+) as: "A multilingual social networking and identity service owned and operated by Google Inc. It was launched in June 28, 2011. As of June 2012, it has a total of 250 million registered users of whom 150 million are active. Unlike other conventional social networks which are generally accessed through a single website, Google has described Google+ as a "social layer" consisting of not just a single site, but rather an overarching "layer" which covers many of its online properties"

Google+ has been on my radar for more than a year and it has certainly evolved as a collection of tools designed to rival social media sites like Facebook and Twitter. It has an impressive 170 million plus users, significantly less than Facebook, but more than LinkedIn and Twitter. Yet when you delve deeper into the figures, you can see the actual usage of Google + trails well behind any of the other social media sites.

There is a great bunch of statistics from Umph — a UK based social media company, that show in real terms the average user of Google+ spends just 3.3 minutes per month on the site compared with 7.5 hours for the average Facebook user (www.umph.co.uk).
However, there does seem to be a lot of evidence that shows a good business based Google+ site linked to your web pages, can help with rankings. I have just started using Google+ linked to my website, so it is early days yet; however I can see how it could potentially help.

Setting Up

If you are going to set up a Google+ account, it is a very simple process. Start by Googling 'Google+' and creating a new account. As always, use the keywords within your account name as far as possible.

In common with other social media there are many ways to make sure that you get the most out of each platform that you use and here are a few tips to get you started.

GET AS MANY GOOGLE+ FOLLOWERS AS YOU CAN

The more followers you have the more importance Google+ will give you; it definitely seems that quantity wins over quality.

SHARE YOUR GOOGLE+ ACCOUNT ON ALL YOUR OTHER SOCIAL MEDIA WEBSITES FOR PEOPLE TO LINK TO

Put a link to your Google+ account or profile on your website, and anywhere else you can use such as your email signature, forums, and social media profiles. Also remember to include your Google+ details when you comment on blogs.

ADD THE GOOGLE+ BADGE TO YOUR WEBSITE

Make sure your profile information and all other web pages are completely filled in; Google can prioritise different areas of your profile in search results

I have found online articles, that show Google+ profiles that are linked to a website, can achieve a higher ranking than those with no link, so it's worth building it into your longer term strategy, certainly there is nothing to lose.

References and Resources

Google+:
https://accounts.Google.com/ServiceLogin?service=oz&continue=
https://plus.Google.com/?gpsrc%3Dgplp0&hl=en.
Umph: http://www.umpf.co.uk/.

STEP 5

CREATE CONTENT

Step 5

"Either write something worth reading or do something worth writing." ~ Benjamin Franklin

Content can mean many things in our digital world: videos, images and articles. Whatever form it takes, as long as it is informative and relevant, people are hungry for it.

We've already looked at images and video and in this section I want to focus on articles that you or someone you hire can write with you or for you to meet this need and establish you as a thought leader.

Original Content

Your first task is to find someone to work with. I found a student who was taking a degree in journalism. The student wasn't an expert in my market but she really knew how to take a bunch of words and mould them into something readable and how to source articles to create blog postings for me.

If I saw a good article in a technical magazine, I could pass it across and the student would research it, adapting it to my market and with the right acknowledgements to copyright, would post it up on my blog for me.

This kept up a regular flow of well written blogs, some challenging, some technical and some just giving top tips, such that over a couple of months we were the number one blog in our industry.

So, visit your local college or university and find some students taking journalism and see if you can find someone to work with, who will like the part-time income and the exposure the blog will give them.

Content Curation

Curation as a word has been around for a while, but only more recently applied to the social media marketplace.

In social media it is the process of taking other people's ideas and bringing them all together so you create something brand new yourself.

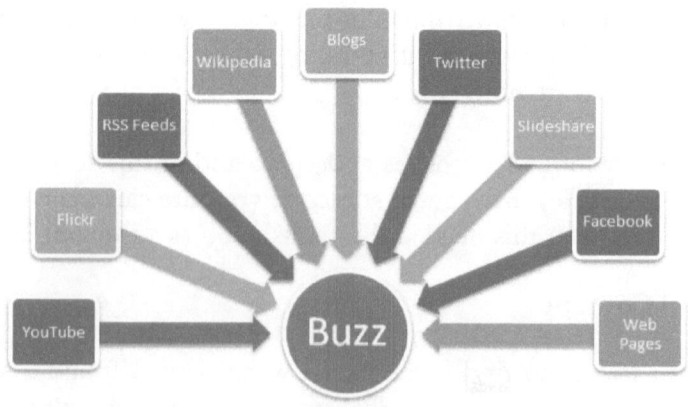

Figure 1

There are a number of online tools that allow you to bring together a 'newsletter' of sorts based on curated content, and that you can then publish to your website, email people or automatically update your Facebook, Twitter and LinkedIn accounts.

Personally, I really like the idea of a curated content newsletter and my favourite, at the time of writing this book, is Scoop.it, which is free to use for most of what you need to do, with a paid for option for the advanced features. To get a picture of it, imagine an online newsletter that you create, with stories, news, video links and commentary, that can be circulated to all your potential customers.

Add to these benefits, the fact that it only takes a fraction of the time to manage compared with a normal newsletter, that you can allow comments, that people can retweet it and that it embeds video such as YouTube really well, and you'll understand why I like it.

Once you create your 'curation' you have the opportunity to create the link across to your Facebook account, where you can share anything from the whole newsletter to a particular article; the same is true for your LinkedIn and Twitter accounts; the latter also provides a shortened URL, which links back to your work. The great thing is that this is picked up by Google and indexed, so your name, your curation title and content then can be found through the search engines.

As an experiment I created a curation of information that I captured from the web, all based around the new Range Rover Evoque, linking to articles that I found of interest. I posted a link to my curation on a couple of forums about the Range Rover and within three days, if you searched on the keywords I used: 'RR Evoque', I came seventh on the first page of Google. Not bad, when you think that Google reported 8.3 million results for that search. Even better, was that within a couple of months, I had over 3000 views of my newsletter, and now I have three out of the top four Google entries for RR Evoque newsletter and one entry on the main Google page for Range Rover Evoque newsletter.

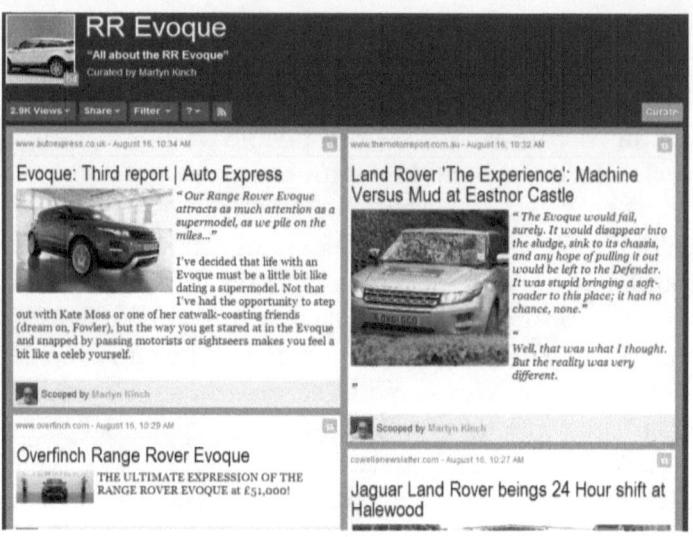

Figure 2

So let's look at how we go about creating a curation of information to support our other promotion activities and if you don't have much to say yourself, don't worry: copy and paste what others are saying.

Firstly, go to the Scoop.it website and create an account. There are a couple of videos to take you through how it all works and how to set up your first curation. When I set up my first try, I just picked on a subject to experiment with and learnt how to use the tools available, plus set up the link to my Twitter, LinkedIn and Facebook account.

Once you get the hang of how it all links together, then pick the subject you want to curate and, again, as much as you can, use the same keywords in your title as we have through the book and again repeat these in the 'tag' tab for each of the articles you bring into your newsletter.

One of the great little tools you will be given the option to install, is a button for your web browser (although I couldn't get this to work on an iPad).When you find a web page or article you want to use, you can press the button and it will 'Scoop.it' the information for you. You can modify any picture (Scoop.it allows you to cycle through the pictures on the web page or upload your own) and edit the text that goes with it, add any tags and publish it.

On your home page on Scoop.it, you can then also use the options underneath each article to move it to where you want to on the page, giving priority to those articles you feel are more relative.

Scoop.it also has its own search function, so it will find links for you to Scoop, either from other Scoop.it users or other suggested links. The best thing to do is to have a play around with the options, and consider how you may best use Scoop.it and its curation tool, to boost your visibility in your chosen market. For along with original content creation, this is yet another way to make you more visible and more successful than your competitors.

I now find that people re-post my tweets that link to my Scoop.it page, and this then brings in more followers to my Twitter account, and they can, of course, follow my Scoop.it account directly.

Amazon and Bookshops

Unlikely as it may seem, internet-bookseller Amazon can be an effective way to generate leads, bring business to you and do that all important thing – establish you as a thought leader in your industry. I figured out a long time ago that when someone wanted to research a subject they looked on the web and they would often start with a book or nowadays with an eBook. Which is where I came in, of course.

Example

In my previous business, based on this premise, I started a bookshop. First, I found the top 10 reference book titles in my market area, then I went direct to the publishers and negotiated a good discount, before going to the online store, EKM Powershop where for a fixed monthly fee I was able to setup a pretty good bookshop which was linked to PayPal, to my credit card merchant account and also to my website.

Next stop was Amazon. All the titles I had were stocked by them anyway, so I set myself up as a market place reseller, created an account and started listing my top seller at a price that was less than Amazon's headline price.

Naturally, I didn't always make a profit - at certain points I was operating at a small loss - but I kept my prices lower than Amazon for a very good reason. Whenever someone bought a book, Amazon would notify me of the purchaser's details so I could ship the book.

Now, I am sure you are already ahead of me, but just to underline it, I now had the contact details of someone interested in the same subjects that I was and therefore in the same market and therefore a potential customer for my business, product or service.

Of course, if you do this you will have the cost of shipping the book purchased, but at this point you could also include a discount voucher for future purchases, a catalogue of your other goods, membership or details of your blog and twitter accounts. The more services that you can offer this new customer of yours, the more likely they are to come back and keep in touch.

Creating your own Amazon Content

Once we had started to ship books through our bookshop, both direct from our website and Amazon, I puzzled over how I could take more control and own something that would be unique to me. I worked out that people like information when researching, and that people in my business liked reference guides, so looking at my own products and services I tried to find a way to create something I could own.

I came up with the 'Process Map'. It showed at a glance how each of my product's stages related to each other and any interdependencies. The reverse of the Map listed all the various documents required and at which point they were used. I had one of our subject matter experts make sure it made sense and had a graphic designer help me lay it out for what would be A3 and A2 size laminated versions.

On the Map I then put my company details, website links, email and telephone contact details. After that it was a question of applying to the Nielsen UK ISBN Agency for an ISBN number and to do an initial run and we were away. We really were; that Process Map brought in so many leads that it paid for itself many times over.

You can do something similar. Think about what you could produce as a handy reference guide that prospects and customers alike would want to put up on a wall, or keep on their desk, or share with their colleagues and refer to on an on-going basis.

Steps for using Amazon

The ISBN process is quite simple and if you Google 'ISBN numbers' you will find the details for your area and the process of application. It can take some weeks to come through, but when it does you will have a unique ISBN number for your document that can be used to register it on Amazon. The application form is pretty straightforward, but remember to use as much as you can, the same keywords in the description and title, as discussed before.

Once the ISBN process is complete, you need to go onto Amazon and set up a Market Place account and register yourself as a trader. All these options are at the bottom of the Amazon home page and registration is very easy. You can then register your publication and by entering the ISBN number, Amazon will bring up your document ready for you to add further details and pricing.

Remember the keywords are very important; you want your item to appear on Amazon every time someone searches on your keywords, preferably in the top couple of items. When you search and find your publication, you will see the comments and review area and further down the page an area that says 'I am the Author/Publisher' – that will enable you to add your own comments.

You can now also create an electronic version for the Kindle and permit people to 'see' inside some pages your publication, although if you do, make sure any images put online are high quality. Just because of the way Amazon works, you will find your new publication listed by them anyway, as it lists pretty much anything with an ISBN, but it will be quoting long delivery times and list price.

So now you have a small bookshop with one of your leading publications undercutting Amazon and generating leads and with your own unique publication. The next step is to raise the visibility of your own publication, for ease of reference, let's refer to it as a process map.

There are many ways to do this. You could use your now sophisticated social media tools to tweet, blog and so on. You could also find some customers to whom you can give away for free, the process maps you've created, in return for reviews on Amazon. The more credible they are, the more people will take notice of them.

You need to be prepared to give away electronic copies for free as well so create a PDF version (which is Adobe Acrobat, and is a universal way of creating and distributing documents) or an infographic. My top tip would be to find a graphic designer that can create a high quality copy.

We have used this technique to great effect. The people to whom we gave our map away got something for free that helped them, and by reviewing the map, they not only increased our credibility, but got themselves some free publicity as well. We were able to publicise those again using our social media presence.

You may be wondering at this point, 'why should I give away something so good for free?' Well, we need to establish ourselves as a knowledgeable expert in our market and the process map, our presence on Amazon and the reviews of credible commentators do just that. Sometimes, to make money, we need to give something away.

Case Studies and White Papers

As you'll understand by now, being perceived as an expert in your chosen field is important and case studies can consolidate the impression we want to give. We know that people want information to help them in their decisions, so the more information you can provide to help with that decision, the more likely you are to be involved in any procurement process at a later stage.

If you are a member of an association and/or accreditation body, they may already have some generic case studies you can use. The association we worked with, had around six case studies and whilst they were available generally we still used them as part of the downloads on our website so that our downloads page was a one-stop shop where people could find everything they needed.

Creating your own Case Studies

A case study is many things depending on the industry you are in, but generally it is a study of a particular subject, product, or service, over a period of time that outlines the impact or results from that for the customer or client.

Typically, you might feature a long term user who can provide details on how they used the product or service and the measurable benefits to them. Of course, it also needs to refer to you or your company to make it specific.

The more case studies you can offer, the more they will support peoples decisions to make you part of their selection process. They are, however, quite time consuming to get together and you may need some help from a marketing professional to interview the customer and pull the details into an agreeable format, but they are very much worth doing because of the credibility they give you. As you build them up, put them into the downloads section of the website, with a short explanation of the contents making sure that potential viewers need to register to access it so that you can capture their details.

- Remember that content is now king.
- Be imaginative in the way you get content.
- Write a book or an eBook, or publish something that potential customers might like.
- Use case studies.

Resources and References

EKM Powershop: http://www.ekmpowershop.com/
Amazon: www.amazon.com
RR Evoque: http://www.scoop.it/t/rr-evoque

STEP 6

MAKE EVENTS PAY

"I am careful with my material and presentation."
~ Shelley Berman

Every organisation is under pressure in these tough economic times to make any event that they hold or attend return a benefit. Here I look at how you can ensure that yours do.

Exhibitions

An exhibition, according to Wikipedia, in the most general sense, is an organised presentation and display of a selection of items. For me, business exhibitions are a platform to showcase products, to network and to meet people. I have setup and run exhibitions all over the world for many years, some great and some not so great, so I thought it worth passing on a few words about my experience to date.

The first place to start is with a little research: check attendance numbers for previous shows, attendee profiles, sponsors, location and of course cost. If you are at a show outside your geographic area, then ensure you can follow up any leads locally. There is no point investing in a show in the USA, if you don't have a local presence or agent, because no matter how great the show seems, follow up will be extremely difficult from the UK.

Example

Back in 2002 we launched a new range of training aimed at the USA. All our research told us we had a unique product into a huge market. We invested in launching at the premier show for our industry and we had hundreds of visitors, all interested in what we had.

Guess how many sales we made from that show? A small amount but nowhere near enough to cover our investment and the two sales we made both companies had UK operations.

Once we returned to the UK, very few returned emails or calls and if we did manage to speak to them they were very polite but said the requirement had gone away. Also, many companies outside the UK cannot dial international numbers.

It took a while to figure out that the reason they didn't want to buy from us was because we were not a US-based company. That's the lesson really – don't invest outside your geographic location until you are able to support the local prospects and customers.

Types of Exhibitions

There are generally three types of shows or exhibitions:

1. A small SIG (Special Interest Group) type show that is usually regional
2. The annual show for a specialist market
3. The large multinational show which may include your market

I generally try and attend the first two, but rarely the last, and would think that it would not produce enough leads to justify the expense unless you were a very large corporate.

The SIG is usually a good way to connect with a smaller regional group. Attendance may be low, but usually the members have useful contacts and are influential in their own local companies. Get one of the usually available low-cost stands or maybe sponsor part of the evening and get to say a few words. They are a very inexpensive way to build your thought-leadership profile and your network. Your market will usually have a trade body that runs a user group or SIGs and if they do it is worth becoming a member; there's generally a trade magazine that you can get full of news and contacts for your market.

The second type of show is a specific industry show for a particular market, such as education, finance, property and IT, to name a few. If you have a product or service that is ready to go to market, then you should consider investing in one of these shows as an exhibitor. I would tend to forget any of the gold and silver 'exhibitor opportunities' but do make sure you try and get the free entry in the show guide.

Exhibition Tips

Through many years of exhibiting I have picked up some top tips that worked for us as a company that always wanted to do things on a budget and I would like to share them with you.

You may have big company budget, but if you don't:

- **Keep it simple.** Pull up posters, for instance, will be fine. On a typical 3m x 2m stand three or four posters will probably fit on them including one poster to the side as well.

- **Legibility.** Make sure that you can read what you offer in a couple of seconds. Too many stands make it complicated and a passing prospect will only spend a second or so to decide if you are of interest to him or her.

- **Have a pod (waist-high table).** This can be used to demonstrate on your laptop, if you use one, and should also have somewhere to put brochures and giveaways. Try and keep one with a lockable door. I can remember someone taking our brochures overnight, probably for a prank, but we never got them back.

- **Product displays and demonstrations.** Make sure you have a clear idea of what you are trying to get prospects to buy. Don't clutter the stand and, where possible in your brochures and marketing materials, demonstrate how it can be used and configured; use pictures as much as you can. Don't assume that someone walking past can figure out the best way to use your product.

- **Prizes.** This normally works well for it gets people to stop at your stand. I usually give away something and have a business card box. Surprising as it may seem, whilst people will not always talk to you they all like to win a prize and of course you have captured their data.

- **Stationery.** Make sure you have prospect recording forms, loads of business cards, staplers, elastic bands, pens, Bluetack and masking tape. All of them will be required at some stage.

- **Give-aways.** Try and find something to give away that people would like and find useful. I gave away the Process Maps that I mentioned earlier. I have also done a deal with a publisher to give away free promotion pocketbooks. I would put all my details on the inside cover and used those to give away and open up conversations. If you do this make sure it is mentioned in the trade entry for the show or on a poster somewhere. I made a great big orange circle about a metre wide with 'free pocket book here' on it and stuck it out in front of my stand. That certainly got people's attention and made them curious!

- **Organisation.** If you have other people helping you, have a team meeting at the start of the day and be clear about what you want from them, stand etiquette, breaks and who does what.

- **Attendance list.** When you negotiate the stand, try to get access to the attendance list as part of the package, some companies will let you have a list of everyone that registered. If not then the prize ideas is well worth considering.

- **Choose the right people to people the stand.** I try to include someone on the exhibition stand that is very outgoing, this works if you find it more difficult to stop strangers and talk to him or her. I used to take my wife with me, who would strike up a conversation with anyone and after a minute or so she would bring them over to me to chat further, whilst she went off and got her next potential client!

- **Keep leads safe – I mean really safe!** We left our leads on the stand in a cupboard overnight at one show and came back the next day to find them all missing. Never let them out of your sight!

- **Enjoy the show.** The more relaxed you can be, the more likely people will come and talk to you. Do not stand like soldiers guarding a fort, if you are a quiet person, sit and use your laptop or write and then catch people when they wander past you and stop to read the posters.

- **Follow up.** Make sure you phone or follow up very quickly once the show is over, many companies despite spending thousands of pounds, are very lax about distributing and following up leads. You will have the edge if you respond within days.

- **Strike while the iron is hot.** A final comment is that of the countless shows I have attended over the years, I have found that the chatty prospect, with a huge potential requirement and the one that we all get excited about, becomes almost impossible to get hold of after the show. Once someone leaves the stand, your chances of doing business decline fast, as your competition also has the same information. If you have a good opportunity just get your diary out and make an appointment there and then to go and see them or create a next step that gives you an edge. If you can do that, then you will be ahead of everyone else.

Seminars and Speaking Opportunities

Seminars work in some businesses, not in others, but it is worth giving some thought to whether a seminar programme could help raise your visibility in your marketplace.

When I talk about seminars, I really mean any opportunity to speak or promote yourself, your company, your products and services in an open forum. As you become recognised for your knowledge in the social world, speaking opportunities will re-enforce this further and will improve your credibility and generate leads.

When we started out in our marketplace, we were very much a minor player in our field and I needed a way to establish both our products and expertise fairly quickly and get those leads. It was time to be canny.

Example

I found a subject matter expert, a hosting company and a supplier (not a competitor) who were in the same market as me. We then tracked down suitable cost-effective premises and set the date. Using our good website and mailing lists we started the campaign to advertise the first 'free' seminar in our market using guest speakers. Over the six weeks that we ran the seminar campaign 50 people registered and on the day over 30 people turned up. Doesn't sound a huge amount, but we were the first company to offer something for free in a relatively immature market.

We were also unusual in that we sold the concept of an expert presenting on our product subject for an hour, of another company talking about tools that would support the products and of the hosting company talking for a couple of minutes about their service. Subtly wrapped around this was the sales pitch, a gentle look at how the product was used and a special show offer to get people to commit. Did we sell anything on the day? No – not on the first one, or indeed the first couple, but as we ran more and more, attendance went up first to 50, then 75 and started averaging at around 100 people at a time and that's when we started taking orders on the day. We didn't sell enough to retire on, but it covered the costs and it delivered the real gold: names and contacts which in later months turned into business.

Making Seminars Work

It's worth reviewing in more detail how we made all this work. The subject matter expert did it for free, as he got a chance to promote himself and his expertise. The tool supplier did it for free, as I was happy for him to share the leads we got. The hosting company did it for free, as I gave them a slot to promote their services (they were an Internet Service Provider, so this was an ideal opportunity).

In our market place, this concept has now been imitated and modified. Some companies charge a small fee; we tried this but the administrative costs and the hassle outweighed the benefits so we partnered with others to control costs. Other companies make it too much of a sales pitch. We still hold some of the best attended seminars in our marketplace all over the world.

I am sure that our success in the following years stemmed from the seminar and speaking programmes. When someone that attended one of our events wanted something in our marketplace, they saw us as an expert in our field and would always include us in their final selection.

The Seminar is a Barometer of Business

The 'seminar' as we all called it, became our barometer of business openings outside the UK as well. To test if we thought there was an opportunity overseas, say in Holland, we would pick a date, find some non-competitive partners in the same market and focus on a date. Attendance and feedback at that seminar would help us evaluate the potential for those products and services in that region.

If I have made this sound too easy, I should explain that it wasn't as I show below but the effort was always worth it.

Example

For some years I had in my mind that Australia was a good market. We set out to find a partner, to jointly invest in a seminar programme. I flew out in 2002 and over the course of 10 days we ran six seminars in six different cities. Attendance was good, but it became clear that it was very early days for that market; we sold some product, but as a result of the feedback, we didn't go back to Australia for another five years. But it could have been worse.

We arrived in Adelaide for one of our seminars, with very small attendance figures, but decided to go ahead anyway. We stayed at a rather cheap and cheerful hotel to keep costs down, which was on the first and second floor above a shop and had stairs leading downstairs straight onto the busy main road.

There were four of us and I was trailing behind coming down the stairs carrying a box of brochures and I tripped – this sent me barrelling down the stairs unable to stop, straight into my co-presenters, with the result that we all came hurtling out of the entrance straight onto the main road, brochures, arms and legs everywhere. We were narrowly missed by more cars than I care to remember, it was one big noise of shouts, tyres screeching and horns. Luckily, although a little bruised, we all survived and went on to present as if nothing had happened. Moral of the story: be prepared for everything and don't give up. We didn't.

In 2007, we ran the same seminar programme (minus of course the stairs incident), and in the space of two weeks sold more product on the day than we ever had in any other seminar worldwide. Now we knew the marketplace was ready.

The result of our 2007 experience was that we sent over one of our best people with nothing more than a suitcase and some products.

We couldn't have written a better sequel if we had tried. The success was phenomenal. Thanks to our holistic selling and marketing techniques, our one-person seminar programme grew to the extent that within 18 months we employed seven people and had a prestigious office on Sussex Street overlooking Darling Harbour. This office became the fastest growing and second largest business outside the UK – all through a couple of exploratory visits using seminars.

There is more to international business than this of course and I go into more detail in the international selling chapter but the point here is that wherever you are in the world, seminars can be a great way of getting a feel of the marketplace and by giving something away for free people will come and see you.

If you are wondering at this stage why you should bother about seminars when we now have webinars (next section), the answer is that each attracts a different kind of buyer. Moreover, in certain circumstances, there is nothing to replace meeting people face to face to develop good long-term business rapport and to increase sales.

Besides, we gave ourselves an extra edge. Through our membership of professional bodies (I discuss this kind of membership elsewhere) we had the opportunity to speak at industry events, take speaking slots at exhibitions and all the while that we were giving our knowledge away for free we were gaining a reputation as experts in our field.

So now it's time for you to consider your own marketplace and ask yourself if there is the opportunity to put together some like-minded people and run some seminars that you all benefit from? Remember what I said before: people crave information to help them make sure they are making the right decision.

Webinars and Web Conferences

A webinar is a 'virtual seminar, workshop or conference on the web that you attend through your smartphone, tablet or computer. It is a cost-effective way of communicating real time with prospects and customers that may be geographically spread out and allows two-way communication between the people connecting into, and the people holding, the conference. Not surprisingly, therefore, there is a trend for more companies to run web conferences and webinars.

If you and your potential customers are based in a country like the UK, with its short distances, face-to-face meetings and webinars are both viable. However, once either you or your market is based outside the UK, then webinars make good sense as a cost-effective way to eyeball prospects or customers.

Webinar Software

Depending on your chosen solution, you may require additional software to be installed by the presenter and participants, however there are many proven applications out there such as Webex, Adobe Acrobat Connect (this has the core features of the previous Connect), Glance and Microsoft Live Meeting to name a few.

If you search on Google for these products, you will find demonstration areas and samples so play around to understand the scope and fit to your business. If you are training, for example, you may have a different requirement to someone that is just showing products or presenting. Most also provide a means of interfacing with email and calendaring clients in order that customers can plan an event and share information about it, in advance.

Web Cast

Where a webinar is only one-way traffic - with the speaker addressing the audience and with limited interaction (like a presentation or a lecture) - it could perhaps more accurately called a 'web cast'. Recently I have been involved in running product training sessions using web casts. It is a great way to get a group of users together to make sure they understand how to use the product to provide on-going training.

Webinars and seminars can both be useful. I have to say, however, that having run both my experience is that while we get high numbers attending webinars, our seminars, even when they have less people, bring in more sales both on the spot and shortly afterwards.

References and Resources

Webex:
https://signup.webex.co.uk/webexmeetings/GB/uk_ft_signup.html?CPM=KNC-sem&TrackID=1021386&semid=s7dmRvbSF_11019846266&psearchID=webex.
Adobe Acrobat Connect Now:
https://www.acrobat.com/main/en/home.html.
Glance: http://www.glance.net/site/index.aspx.
Microsoft Live Meeting: http://office.microsoft.com/en-gb/live-meeting-help/.

STEP 7

MARKET YOUR COMPANY

Step 7

"The aim of marketing is to know and understand the customer so well the product or service fits him and sells itself." ~ Peter F. Drucker

Throughout this book, my aim has been to help you understand and reach your potential customer. The techniques, approaches and my quick guide to marketing below, make up some of the tools that will help you achieve that end.

Web Testimonials

Testimonials are a great way for current customers to endorse your product or service so that you can attract potential customers. And while its importance may come under the 'very obvious' category, you will be surprised how many businesses do not capitalise on the customers they have.

If I buy online, I am personally quite influenced by testimonials and feedback and I take them into account when I book a hotel room, buy a book, a washing machine, a car, pretty much everything these days. And as more purchases are made online, you have to give your potential customer a good feeling about what they are going to invest their money in so they feel comfortable making the choice.

I like to think of a sale as being made up of a number of tick boxes, none of which particularly influence the sale alone, but together make a very powerful argument to buy. Testimonials are part of that chain, a mental tick in the prospect's head that other people that are happy with the outcome use your product or service.

Testimonials from happy clients are an important part of your website and any supporting documentation such as brochures for example can lend trustworthiness and experience to a business. They show your customer that independent third parties value your product and service.

Display

Once you have got your testimonials, how you display them can make a difference. They can be displayed in many ways, in quotes, images and quotes, speech bubbles, audio or video based. As before, look around on the web, look at how other companies do it and find a style that suits you.

I always prefer to keep it simple, a nice explanation of three or four lines in quotes with the name of the person and/or company next to it. These could be on the right hand side of a website in a scrolling box, with a link to all testimonials or at the bottom of any web page concerned with purchasing; it really is down to personal preference and design. The key is to have them in the first place!

Sourcing Testimonials

This is not as hard to do as you might imagine. If a customer ever tells you how much they value your service or asks what they can do for you, ask them for a testimonial. In fact, even if they don't, ask anyway. They really are that valuable to you.

In the early days we would trade testimonials for discount. If someone wanted to negotiate on price, I would ask them that if they liked our product, they would in return give us feedback we could use. This is not always easy with corporate customers, where any comment may have to go back through some authorisation within the company, but persevere as corporate endorsement is worth its weight in gold.

A couple of rules are worth mentioning here. Never, ever, fake your reviews; most sensible people can spot them a mile away. Always use testimonials that fit the area you are promoting and do not over edit them, the quote should flow almost in a conversational way.
If you can quote specifics in the testimonial they work really well, so for example "we made savings of over ££", "productivity increased xx%", you can see the sort of thing I am suggesting, so try and get it specific for your particular market.

If you don't have any testimonials, go and see existing customers; you will be surprised how much they want to help you succeed, as your success ensures continued support and development for existing and new products in the future. Everyone wants to be part of something successful.
If you are brand new, starting from scratch, then perhaps drop back to testimonials about you; LinkedIn is a great personal reference tool, which makes it easy to ask for testimonials from friends and colleagues. Take these and reference them in your marketing to at least establish yourself as a product or service worth investing in.

Evaluations, Pilots, Samples and Give-Aways

After many years of trying to decide what to give and show prospects and what to keep back, I have got to a point where I think I know what works well and I hope this can work for you in the same way.

Sometimes people want to try before they buy and I have to say in the software world this is a little easier than in most industries, particularly if you have to buy product in. However, the principle stands that if you can loan or pilot your goods or service, it can be a differentiator with your competitors.

Because of what we sold, which was software based, quite often a large corporate would want to purchase a single user licence to pilot or review the course, prior to maybe or maybe not taking it any further. Well I figured that if they purchased just one licence then I would lose control over their evaluation, I would have to wait for them to come back to me, which could be never.

We decided that if a corporate customer wanted to evaluate our product, then we would give them a free copy. Then we kept more control over when the evaluation started, how long it would last and feedback at the end of the trial. One of the golden rules of doing this was that once a date was agreed to start the evaluation and if within a short period the user had still not started, then we would withdraw the evaluation and offer to start it again once the user had free time.

This gave value to the trial period and we kept control of the process. After all, unless there was a pretty good excuse, then it obviously was not that important to them and most likely would be a waste of our time to put too many resources into the sale.

Depending on what product you have, ask yourself if you can afford to offer a pilot or free trail for a short period. Or you could offer a voucher that gives a discount for the initial purchase or a credit that can be used against a future purchase.

You need to base your decision on your situation. For instance, in our market, if a customer wanted to purchase a larger number of licences to pilot then often I would offer a credit for the total cost of the pilot against a future purchase, within an agreed timescale. At least you can retain some control over timing using that approach.

Business Cards

There are plenty of stories about the origins of business cards: they came from the East; they originated in the visiting cards used in the court of Louis XIV of France; they were trade-cards used in England. Whatever their true origin they have played a part in introducing and advertising businesses and individuals for many years.

In this internet age, a lot of businesses underestimate the power of the humble business card and what it can do for them. Your business card represents you in the same way that all the other elements in my book do – they create your first impression, they are your contact tool, your referral and the way that potential customers will find you after a show, presentation or seminar.

So make sure you create something that looks good, something that contains everything the potential customer needs to contact you and you will find it really can be the difference between success and failure.

Here are some tips to help you create the best business card you can for your particular business.

Avoid Home-Made Cards

Please avoid these at all costs; they look homemade and in many cases if they get slightly wet, then the ink will run all over - more than likely on the customer's hands or suit or dress! The cost of cards has dropped dramatically over the years, so, with a little thought and planning, there is no reason you cannot create a card that gives you the edge over your competition.

Make an Immediate Impression

I tell my team that when creating the business card, they should work on the basis that if someone found it on the floor, when they picked it up, they would be able to see what we do and be impressed enough to call us. Another way would be to look at business cards pinned to a board, if there are thirty of forty cards, would yours stand out?

So many cards just contain the company contact details, imagine being at a show and collecting dozens of cards with those on, when you look back a week later how can you remember which company did what? A potential customer is likely to start with the cards that clearly explain what the company does.

Customise and Create

Your potential customer will see numerous business cards during their travels so make your card a memorable one. Put on your creative thinking cap and customise every detail of your card according to the audience you are marketing to and the services you are marketing. Anyone can hand out a standard business card but the professional who expresses their organisation's message and personality through their card will have the edge on the competition. Unlike the old days, cards can be customised easily online so you won't have to leave your home or office.

Avoid Flimsy Cards

The weight and texture of your card is the first thing someone notices when it is handed to them. Handing out a thin, flimsy card will signal that you put little thought and even less effort into the development of it. Use high-quality cards with a glossy or matte finish for a sharp look that will call your audience to action. You can also use portrait-style or vertical business cards to stand out among your competitors.

Use the Back of your Card

It's important to give your business card as much leverage as possible, so use all available space, including the back (obviously don't overdo it). For while the back content should be secondary in importance to contact information, options include calendars, appointment cards, product information, customer testimonials or quotes from your company's leader. Business cards are small and supply a limited space but it is important space. Don't waste it.

Add a Face to the Name

Adding your photo to a business card can be a great way to build professional relationships, especially if you're working in an industry such as an estate agency where a personal touch is important. Trust is the key to a lasting and profitable business relationship and giving your organisation a face can help this along.

Go Back to Basics

It may seem obvious, but some companies fail to list all the necessary information on their business cards. The basic elements of a business card include name, title, company name and website address and all relevant contact information, including fax number, Skype details, Twitter name, Facebook page and any blog details (as relevant, of course). Lead with your company's name and, space permitting, include a clear, concise positioning statement or tagline.

Colourful Cards

The colour of your card should be tailored to the type of business you represent and your target audience. Warm and inviting colours, such as blue and white, are perfect for a doctor's card, while an artist or entertainer may go with a black card to display their off-beat creativity. Make sure your cards are full-colour to cast a bright, eye-catching image but do avoid using hard-to-read yellow business cards.

QR Codes

A quick response (QR) code is a two-dimensional, black and white coloured code that a smartphone can read and then transfer information. You see them everywhere now and they need to be seen on your business cards so potential customers can read your contact details, be directed to your website, blog or Facebook page and can even get a discount that you may be offering.

Different Cards for Different People

Businesses that market to a wide-ranging audience should consider creating more than one card design for personnel. Your company needs to be all things to all people so why not have multiple card designs when you have to influence very different audiences with very different needs? The small amount of money spent developing the additional cards will pay for itself in the form of the extra business gained.

This is particularly true when working outside your home country. I typically had three cards: one that had dual addresses on such as a UK card with an Arabic translation on the reverse, one that was just for the UK, and one with no title.

Example

It's worth sharing with you why I had a card with no title on it. Think back to what I've been saying about perception being reality. In selling you have to assume a number of roles, it doesn't matter particularly if you actually are the CEO and/or the sales manager. I would adapt my role according to the customer I was selling to; I wanted to be at the level that made me the least threatening. At times my managing director card stayed firmly in my card case as it could have intimidated and created a barrier with certain levels of buyer. At other times it was this card that I got out for certain customers and that got doors opened for me.

My favourite ploy when selling was just to introduce myself as a field sales person and during negotiation I would say that I needed to get my manager's sign off for a discount or deal and then ask that if I could get the sign off would they go ahead? I would then contact them to say I had got sign off, but only until the end of the week or month, so we needed to move quickly. But of course there was no manager – just me negotiating with myself and putting myself on the customer's side. Simple but it worked and it's back to the power of having the right business cards.

The other time the blank card came in handy was on the only presentation that anyone ever complained about me. Having travelled quite a long way to a company presentation, I had gone through the technical details and the company had previously told me they had budget and sign off for the project, only to announce that the budget had been stopped. At this point I pretty much started to wind up the presentation and left.

About a month later someone called in to speak to the sales director and I took the call. It was the same company I had previously presented to, wanting to talk further but complaining about the 'salesperson who came and once they realised we had no budget they closed their briefcase and left'.

Well of course I promised to find out who it was and make sure they were disciplined over the matter and I would get someone else to deal with them. Once they were happy with that, I sent over one of my other salespeople, who took an order and slapped myself on the wrist for being a little too fast to leave the presentation – thanks goodness I had used my blank title business card!

Font Size Matters

Never use a font smaller than 8-10 point on your business card. Cards that have readers reaching for a magnifying glass will only cause frustration. While it's great to be stylish, avoid using an ultra-fancy font that's on the verge of being illegible. Make sure the print on your card blends properly with its background colour and design.

Brag About Yourself

Tell the world if you and your organisation have won awards. Proudly list any awards on the front or back of your card as it can only enhance your contact's interest in doing business with you. Whether you are an MD or PhD, list your qualifications and professional status. It won't take up much space and it will signal that you are knowledgeable and experienced.

Don't Break the Bank

Business cards are worth every penny but you don't have to spend a chunk of your marketing budget on them. Search for free business card offers and enlist the services of a company that can produce high-quality yet affordable cards. If you're a small or home business owner, work with a company that allows card orders in small business-friendly quantities. It's also worth adding that I like to find something someone else has done and build on that for myself. So look at all the business cards in your collection and see any you like and start from that base.

MailShots

Mailshots are where you send out mail in bulk to advertise your products and services. There has been a huge shift in the way mailshots work and what is 'sent' out as technology moves us from paper into the electronic world we live in today.

When we started out in business, it was the norm to send out letters in the post, usually in a full A4 size envelope with usually one or two attachments. We would try (and it didn't always work!) to convince the children it was a game to stuff envelopes and a wet Sunday afternoon could be made fun by seeing who could 'stuff' the most envelopes. In all honesty, it was cheap labour, but we needed to get our message out into the market and even now our children remind us of those lost weekends!

Not much has really changed, but the prohibitive cost of the same mailing that we undertook, has meant a shift towards email mailshots the overuse of which has created what we know and love as spam.

Data Protection Act UK

It's worth just running through some of the rules that govern what you can, and cannot do, with data that you keep in your business which is governed by the Data Protection Act in the UK. Bear in mind, I am only giving you an outline here so you should get advice from the appropriate department and website.

When you deal with individuals you have to ensure you do several things:

- Tell them who you are
- Tell them what you will use their information for

Share anything else necessary to make sure you are using their information fairly, including whether you plan to pass your marketing lists to other organisations and how you will be contacting people, such as by post, phone or email

When you collect information from people you are in direct contact with, such as in a phone call or on a website, you should give them an immediate opportunity to object to future contact. You could also find out how they would like to be contacted in future.

Permission means that people requested email marketing from you. Before investing your time and money in an email-marketing program, start getting permission from your customers.

It's easier than you think and it'll result in fewer spam complaints, better deliverability, decreased legal liability and **--most importantly--** better open and click results. Most good mail programmes such as MailChimp automatically asks for a permission reminder in your campaigns.

Mailing Lists

A popular option to expand markets is to purchase, either as a rental or full ownership, a mailing list that everyone has 'opted in' and is happy to be contacted. There are hundreds of companies offering this service, so I would start with the magazines and exhibitions that are in your market, generally the companies that run these will rent a list of subscribers or registrants. Try trade associations too for they may have an option to send some form of communication to other members.

132

You can usually purchase by a number of variables and I guess it depends very much on your business as to what is applicable, but the most common are:

- Employee size or company turnover
- Geographic area
- Job title
- Type of business
- Specialty
- Headquarters and branches
- Telephone numbers

SIC Codes

A SIC Code means a "Standard Industrial Classification", that describes the Industry Groups that companies are put into. You can Google SIC codes for a complete list and it can make it easier to say target Banks, which would be a SIC code starting 60XX, where the last two digits describe the sub category.

So in our fictitious company called Welearnmore, we may want to purchase a list with the job titles 'project manager' & 'training manager' in the UK, with more than 100 employees. We then need to ask questions and get information. We would ask mailing companies to give a record count of how many people they have in that category.

Then we would ask to see some sample records, which they should supply. To check on the quality of what we get we could do LinkedIn searches or perhaps call the switchboard of the company.

Finally, we would get a price for how much it will cost, bearing in mind that the company may want to do the mailing themselves (common with magazines) or we may be able to purchase a single use or unlimited use licence. The companies have also figured how to make more money by charging you extra for a phone number or email address, so make sure you know what you are purchasing.

Email Mailshots and Newsletters

I would say that the majority of people that do outbound marketing use email mailshots and newsletters at some point. Providing you have met the requirements of the Data Protection Act and have an 'unsubscribe' button or link in your mailshot, then you are ready to go!

Having sent hundreds and possibly thousands of mailings over the many years I have been in business, I have a personal feel for what works and what doesn't and although what works for me may be different for you and for your products and services, there are some tips that are helpful for all.

Content Based Newsletters

People like information, as you no doubt tire of me telling you. So if you are in a particular industry and every month you get a newsletter updating you on new events, then you are likely to forgive any subtle advertising. It also adds to your credibility as making you look as though you are well informed and knowledgeable. However, most of us dislike full-on sales newsletters and out-and-out spam so try to avoid it if you can otherwise you may end up with lots of unsubscribe requests rather than enquiries.

If your newsletters are great your readers will communicate with you on social networks and help you spread the word. Keep providing good content in your campaigns and maybe even let them behind the scenes of your company. When you truly engage your subscribers - by answering their questions, solving their problems, meeting their needs and listening to their feedback - they'll feel appreciated.

Email Address

Don't send a big email campaign to your customers and use your "@yahoo.com" or "@aol.com" home email address. Use instead your website's domain - you should already have email accounts set up under that domain. Some people like setting up an additional newsletter@companydomain.com address for their emails.

Cultural Differences

It's worth adding there are cultural differences as well, so what may work here, may not work so well in another country. A good lesson for me was when we took our marketing model to Australia and used the same methods we used in the UK. Suddenly we found we were getting complaints and unsubscribes; a few phone calls later, we realised Australians do not like receiving mailshots in the same frequency as people do in the UK. So in Australia we sent half as many and made them informative and that worked. So remember there may be obvious as well as subtle differences in the way people do business in other countries.

Newsletter Appearance

Your newsletter or mailshot needs to look good, and you absolutely need to do some test mailshots for what looks good on your screen can translate badly in extra linefeeds on another computer.

Email Packages

Use a professional package if you can to handle your mailings, so that 'unsubscribe' requests and bounce back from dead emails can be handled automatically.

It may be tempting to handle mailing lists via a spread sheet, but having done this I learnt the hard way that when we needed to transfer it into a proper prospect management system it was very time consuming. Better to get it right from the beginning.

There are many email packages on the market, I have started to use Google and the 'Cloud' to keep my contacts together, a free customer relationship management (CRM) package called Insightly, Google Mail and, finally, an email package called MailChimp which has about one million users so is well established. All these products have cost plans, but generally for businesses starting out the services are free.

By tying all the information together, my contacts in the CRM system are also available in my Google mail account and MailChimp integrates into these so I can pick and mail most variations of my contact database very easily and also get reports back on how well it is all going.

The MailChimp package also allows you to create good-looking newsletters and the option I like is the Email Inspector which allows you to see what your email will look like. It also has an iPhone app, which makes my life easier, particularly as you can track major clients and their responses.

I wouldn't do a cover design - there are hundreds of templates available that you can use as a base structure for creating the mailshot and if you stick to a clean and simple approach, you will be certainly one up on your competition.

If you Google 'Email Clients' you will see hundreds of packages available, just take your time, read some reviews and feedback and then shortlist what you think works for you.

Most packages offer a 30-day free trial and you can get an idea of how well they work in your industry.

There will be times when you are too busy to do a newsletter or you may be running out of content, remember what I said earlier in the book about finding a student or graduate that can collect information for you, so you have a regular stream of information coming through.

Social Media Mailshots

I think it's worth touching on one big change in mailshots and that is the integration into social media. Using MailChimp as an example, your mailshots can also be posted to your Twitter and Facebook accounts, which means that your followers will hopefully post to their followers and so on. If you add Facebook and Tweet buttons to your mailshot, then there is a chance that your email customers will 'like' it or send it on and Twitter followers will tweet it to people they know.

Depending on your package you should then get reports on how many re-tweets you have or how many Facebook 'likes' you have and who these came from. This feedback allows you to customize future campaigns and target markets.

If your newsletter is informative and relevant there is a chance it will be picked up and re-tweeted and the opportunities that can come from this are huge, as you get recommended into complete new social circles.

This also forms part of the knowledge authority we are trying to create and as we have said previously search engines will pick this up in their searches and your 'authority' in your market will increase.

Links

There are lots of great websites that can help you think through who you are targeting, what message you are trying to create and provide lots of 'do and don't' rules, here are a few that are recommended by MailChimp:

- **BtoB Magazine:** www.btobonline.com: email and direct mail news. Check their "email marketer insight" section.
- **Clickz:** www.clickz.com: lots of email marketing news.
- **Duct Tape Marketing:**
  www.ducttapemarketing.com/weblog.php John Jantsch's Duct Tape Marketing Blog is full of quick, simple and affordable marketing ideas for business. His book's a great read for businesses that are just getting started.
- **Email Marketing Reports:** www.email-marketing-reports.com Mark Brownlow has posted hundreds of useful email-marketing articles and links here.

- **Email Marketing Typepad:**
- www.emailmarketing.typepad.com Tamara Gielen's blog on email marketing.
- **Future Now Inc:** www.futurenowinc.com: look for their little alien mascot and sign up for their Grokdotcom newsletter. They specialize in conversion and they know their stuff.
- **MailChimp:** www.mailchimp.com/blog - they feature email design tips and tricks, hacks, troubleshooting tips and news.
- **Marketing Experiments:** www.marketingexperiments.com - great experiments and case studies.
- **Marketing Sherpa:** www.marketingsherpa.com - great email marketing case studies and research.

Using Surface Mail

Not too many years ago, I would regularly post 15,000 plus letters in a quarter and get a reasonable response. Of course all that has changed, as electronic mailshots have taken over and all our bills and statements moved to being available online.

In the last two years, I have certainly received significantly less post than I used to and that's the opportunity I want to highlight. For now, when I do receive something in the post with my name on I tend to open it and digest it more than I would have five years ago.
Although most people think of surface mailing as being old hat, I think there is now a niche for people that can still use it in their business.

How to Use Surface Mail Today

If you have a good mailing list, you should consider using it as part of your overall strategy, because very few of your competitors are likely to mail, you have more chance to stand out with your offer or news.

Research from Royal Mail shows that people can spend up to 10 minutes reading mailshots. They digest the information in their own time and at their own pace and then decide to act or not.

The same rules apply as to our electronic mailshots, the first and most important thing is to have a compelling reason for your potential customer to respond (a fantastic offer - only available through mail, for a limited period only), and then, (very important) provide the customer with the easiest way to respond.

The UK Royal Mail has a good section on developing campaigns and also tools to help you create and manage a campaign and responses, you can find out more information at: www.royalmail.com/marketing-services

The Cloud

One of the great changes happening today is about where information is stored; people often refer to this new storage place as the 'cloud'. It's worth covering this briefly if you are setting up a business from new, because it can save you the headache of supporting local software in your office and we have certainly found benefits from using it.

The cloud is essentially called that because your information and the applications required to run them are held on remote computers, in many different locations around the world.

What it means to you and me is that we no longer need to maintain expensive servers and software, as long as we (and potentially our team) have Internet access we can access our information and programme's from anywhere in the world. It keeps costs fixed and gives you security of data and automatic back-up and recovery should anything go wrong with the remote computers.

Google Email and Small Businesses

Of course technically it's a lot more detailed than that, but the principle of starting with something like Google Mail (and yes, you can use your own email address as well), adding many of the thousands of apps (many which are free, such as pipeline management, invoicing and payroll) and having them all talk to each other is a huge benefit.

Google has recently launched a new small business package that allows you to run a whole range of online tools, there is a free version and a paid for version for slightly more flexibility. Google 'Google small business' for more information.

Press Releases

Publicity is the deliberate attempt to manage the public's perception of a subject, says Wikipedia. So for us, in our efforts to make sure our products and services are seen in a positive way, it is important. Although it very much depends on your business, investing in public relations or PR can be quite expensive and time consuming. Any typical agency is likely to want a fixed commitment from you in terms of spend per month and at least a three- month contract.

What we can do, however, is make the most of the tools available to us that are free or very low cost, to maximise any publicity. The internet has created a whole range of free sites that offer to release your news. On the one hand, this makes it easier to broadcast news; on the other, it also becomes much harder, as you are competing with a huge amount of information being posted daily.

Most of what I will cover is designed for online PR websites but, and it's a big BUT, remember that in your industry you will have trade magazines, who will often trade some column inches against an advert or feature. If this is the case, then see if you can afford a small supporting advert in the back of the magazine, this gets you talking to the staff at the magazine, which then builds the relationship through to editorial. Given that it may only be a small handful of trade magazines in your industry, then targeted email mailshots may also work and we can discuss this at the end of the chapter.

It's worth reflecting on a couple of the side benefits of using good PR sites. Remember we talked about the threads that pull all the parts of this book together? Well PR sites will list your entry with Google and whilst you may not get the front page in the Telegraph, your name, company, product and service will appear in searches that potential and existing customers make which, given that many people now get their information from the internet rather than from newspapers as we know them, will probably work in your favour.

The key part of this is to use 'good' sites – there are many PR sites online and the ranking of these will change over time - so do your own research to see what PR site applies to you and your business, and then do some Google searches to see how they appear, and in what priority order. Typically a search on Google for 'free press release' will bring back pages of options, but remember the higher Google ranks them, the more important you should consider them.

Once you have created a press release, then link back to it from your web page; linking to a good, high-ranking PR site from your website helps with the page rank as we explained earlier. If Google can see that high-ranking existing sites link to you, then it will ensure you a higher ranking and obviously even better if you can get a reciprocal link from that PR site back to you. All part of the link building we discussed earlier.

Once you've found a good PR site you obviously need a good press release, and I think it's worth running through some tips for creating good ones; I speak from experience. I used to do all my own with predictably varying results and learned in time that there is good practice that should be followed and that is fairly easy to follow. All you need to do is improve on existing techniques rather than start from scratch.

Research

See what the competition does, look at different styles, see what seems to work in your industry. If you are using a particular site then look at the tone of writing as well as the style and make yours as relevant as possible.

Don't Just Duplicate

Don't just duplicate the same release across each site – this could have a negative effect on your Google rankings. If you want to submit to multiple sites then change the headlines and as much as you can, move around the content a little.

Relevance

Make sure the content has relevance to where you are putting it, don't take a 'shotgun' approach of just firing, hoping that you will eventually hit something.

Headlines

Headlines should be as short and interesting as possible. A good rule would be to keep it short enough for the same release as a 'tweet' including the link. The more eye-grabbing and contentious you can make the headline, the higher the chance of getting it picked up.

Ask For Advice

Get friends or colleagues to give their opinions as well. When you are in the woods, it's difficult to see for trees, so what you think is riveting may be boring and far too technical. Ask yourself, 'why should people care about this?'

Avoid Nonsense Terms

No matter how attractive and tempting they seem, avoid terms, such as 'highly scalable', 'end-to-end solutions', 'strategic partnership', 'best-kept secret'– just keep it simple!

Summarise

Make a summary of what you are selling as soon as you can in the release using the 'who, what, where, when, why' formula.

Once you are done, put it one side for a bit, reflect and then come back and have a last look. Often the summary paragraph at the end is the very one you should have had at the beginning! Oh and try and fit it onto one page or two at absolute maximum.

Quotes

If you can get a really good quote from a customer for your press release, make sure that it can be validated and more importantly, that the person you quoted is willing to take a call from a journalist if required.

Beware of Case Studies

Although case studies are important in their place, my personal view is that they shouldn't be part of your PR. A good journalist once told me that he deletes them all, as do his colleagues, so keep them for use in other areas of the business.

Images

Fancy graphics and big pictures just make a huge attachment. Most journalists who like a release, will ask for pictures. If your release does require a picture or two it's worth spending some money to make sure they look good and professional.

One of the first things did when we launched our new offices was to pay a newspaper photographer to come and take a series of pictures. It was eye-wateringly expensive for us as a small business, but the angle of the shots, the quality and composition were really good, as he knew what a magazine would look for, and it proved to be money well spent. We got some of our press releases picked up, they requested pictures, which we sent over and we got our article in the local press. I am sure that was due to the quality of the supporting pictures we supplied. Many years later we still use many of them, particularly head-shots and have never had one returned or not used.

Contact Details

Finally, make yourself very easy to contact. Remember to put all your contact details down, not just an email or web address and if you are going to be away, ensure you have a plan B to cover you. You are likely to only get the one call and have a short window to respond.

A Quick Guide to Marketing

We have previously covered many techniques of raising the visibility of ourselves, our products and services, and all those form the marketing plan that makes us more successful. You may not need all the elements that we have discussed, but any combination will give you an edge.

I have mentioned elsewhere that one of the things that made a difference to our business was ensuring that we understood our buyers and their motivations. Why did they purchase from us? What was the drive or motivation for that purchase? Why today and not yesterday or tomorrow? Once we started to understand that we could focus down on specific campaigns or social media strategy to ensure we became part of the solution for other people considering the same thing.

And this works right across the world, no matter what industry you are in. If you are a new business then focus on the competitors that you want to beat, why do people buy from them, if it's possible purchase their product or service or sit in their café or buy from their retail store. Just see what it is that motivates people to use them. Is it reputation, price or location, if you were a customer would you buy from them?

Example

We used combined marketing to help a family member establish himself in a new marketplace. He was struggling with work, which was carpentry and cutting his rates to the point that he was barely making a living in a very competitive marketplace. However, I knew we could help him and that all he needed was an 'edge'. And that's what we gave him.

I used a virtual telephone company, AQL, to provide a local number, which diverted to his mobile. We then put an advert into the local paper and decided the theme was 'local' carpenter' which of course linked to a local telephone number. We set him up within Google so he appeared on Google Places, which was free and with a small Adword that was triggered on the keyword 'carpenter Nantwich' which cost very little as there were no competitive paid-for ads. We created a website, uploaded pictures of previous work, references, enquiry form and general contact information. I also got some nice magnetic signs made up, which are very reasonable and they went on the sides and rear of his van, again following the theme local carpenter, time served. I have to say that he also went one stage further and got some t shirts made in bright orange that had his name, telephone and website details on.

Well, it was a big success. Within a week the phone was ringing and besides some small jobs, he picked up an eight week building project. One year on, he has some great long term contracts and has never been happier. George now has a number one position on Google Places and regularly receives two or three calls a day asking for quotes for work. All he needed was a focused campaign with a nice, clear and simple message and it worked.

Now before I go any further, I need to hold up my hands and admit I only understand marketing from a 'sales' view. I have heard people call us a 'sales-led company' rather than a 'marketing-led company' and I think the difference is probably down to the size of company.

For to be a 'marketing-led company' means that you are more than likely a corporate and that your lead generation is run by marketing rather than directly by sales. There are two famous and opposite quotes I like that summarise it very well:

"Marketing consists of individual and organisational activities that facilitate and expedite satisfying exchange relationships

in a dynamic environment through the creation, distribution, promotion and pricing of goods, services and ideas."

"Marketing is too important to leave to the marketing department."

The second quote was from Bill Packard, from Hewlett Packard fame, and my personal favourite. I meet so many companies that 'hand over' their marketing to a marketing specialist who may be a great marketer but who doesn't understand the market. You can be the world's best knowledge expert on using marketing techniques but the important bit is to try and understand the buyer's motivation and link the process back to the sales.

Example

I have done some work with a local café called Enzo which moved into my town around a year ago. It became my favourite place to sit quietly for an hour or two putting my notes together for my book. It was my favourite because it had free Wi-Fi, served great coffee, good service and it was mostly empty first thing in the morning.

During the times that I was there, I became friendly with the team and came to realise that because it was empty, it was in fact not taking enough revenue to ensure it stayed open and met its budgets. The café featured highly in Google, the Tripadvisor reviews were good, but of course it really didn't make much difference to local people, as it seemed to be more passing trade.

I wondered if any of the strategies we had discussed with the book would work; it had a good website, looked good inside the café and out and served great coffee and food. Now we knew that business was there, because there were other local coffee shops that were busy, so the question was how did we get these local people to come to there instead?

So the café owner, James Skade, created a Facebook account started posting up on a regular basis pictures and notes about what was going on. Of course a good Facebook page needs people, so the next step was to advertise in the café the Facebook account, which attracted 'friends' who recommended to their friends.

A competition was also started so that every month free vouchers were awarded for the best picture posted that showed some element of the café – perhaps a picture of a group of friends drinking coffee or some cakes or food. The details of the competition were posted up on some laminated cards that were next to the menu on each table and over a couple of months the number of 'friends' increased dramatically.

The use of QR codes helped, as customers could scan the code, which took them directly to the correct web pages. Outside the café, the signage was changed and now within a second of walking past you could see what they offered, supported by chalk board menus that gave it the 'home made food' feel.

The next thing was to figure out how to get the spend per person increased as two people drinking only coffee over 20 to 30 minutes was not maximizing the opportunity. So next to the Facebook laminate card was put specials such as 'brownies and ice cream' and more work was done on training staff to upsell from a coffee to a coffee and cake or sandwiches or lunch, depending on the time of day. Menus were changed and pictures posted up on Facebook showing a special pizza or coffee and inviting feedback.

Within a couple of months, the worst thing ever had happened, I could no longer get a quiet seat in the morning, because the majority of time the café was packed out, my little oasis of calm was gone, but in its place was a buzzing and busy café.

The café plans to do more. The team has created videos of its cooking to post on YouTube, it's pinning up pictures on Pinterest, it's tweeting some of the specials and keeping special offers, competitions and pictures coming. James is now looking at how he could franchise out the concept or open more cafes using a similar model.

It would be fair to say they have one of the best social media programmes in the area, they engage their customers and make them feel part of the buzz and excitement and they are successful.

James said, *"Essentially, we have found Facebook fits really well with our industry. A cafe or restaurant serves a community as it is a place to get together. Facebook is an online community which allows people to connect digitally so we realised they marry really well."*

"The key thing we have learnt is 'engagement and reach'. We found that there is a direct relationship between the two in social media. We engage with our friends or followers by connecting whether it be through tweets, retweets, conversations on Facebook or photographs because food is SO visual."

"When we do this it extends our reach opening our communication lines further. The 'photo' competition we run every month is very good for us for 2 reasons: people are putting content up (photos) free of charge and showing off our food; they tag us (so it goes on our page) and themselves so all of their friends see it (extending our digital reach)."

"We now use Facebook to serve the local community. I'm now looking to entice every single friend of an existing Facebook customer into Enzo to spend money because they are nearly all local. With Twitter, I'm not looking so much to generate immediate revenue from that, but to further increase brand awareness and engage people on a 1-2-1 basis and make our customers feel that little more special."

As I hope you will agree, I think the café is a good example of what I have been trying to show you, as it shows what I always say – you don't need to be twice as good as the competition, you just need the edge.

So take some time to sit down, look at who you want to be like or who you want to beat, identify their competitive strengths and weaknesses, look at their customers and find out their motivations to buy. And then plan to focus in on them.

- Use the range of tools available in your marketing tool box.
- Adapt traditional techniques so that they work today.
- Be imaginative

References and Resources

BtoB Magazine: www.btobonline.com: email and direct mail news. Check their "email marketer insight" section.

Clickz: www.clickz.com: lots of email marketing news.

Data Protection Act: http://www.ico.gov.uk/for_organisations/data_protection.aspx.

Duct Tape Marketing: www.ducttapemarketing.com/weblog.php John Jantsch's Duct Tape Marketing Blog is full of quick, simple and affordable marketing ideas for business. His book's a great read for businesses that are just getting started.

Email Marketing Reports: www.email-marketing-reports.com Mark Brownlow has posted hundreds of useful email-marketing articles and links here.

Email Marketing Typepad: www.emailmarketing.typepad.com Tamara Gielen's blog on email marketing.

Future Now Inc: www.futurenowinc.com: look for their little alien mascot and sign up for their Grokdotcom newsletter. They specialize in conversion and they know their stuff.

Mail Chimp: www.mailchimp.com/blog - they feature email design tips and tricks, hacks, troubleshooting tips and news.

Marketing Experiments: www.marketingexperiments.com - great experiments and case studies.

Marketing Sherpa: www.marketingsherpa.com - great email marketing case studies and research.

Royal Mail: www.royalmail.com/marketing-services.

STEP 8

SELL LIKE A PRO

Step 8

"Everyone lives by selling something."
~ Robert Louis Stevenson

"Your most unhappy customers are your greatest source of learning." ~Bill Gates

You can have the best product in the world, you can have the best website, you can have the best social media presence but the bottom line is...the bottom line. So, for this most essential aspect of any business, I have brought together some tips that have worked for me in my businesses.

Sales Cycle

Although I would recommend everyone to take a basic course in selling, there are some common tips that I think work in the majority of businesses.

Be Open, Be Honest and Listen

I mentioned earlier that I have been successfully selling since I was 18 years old and the single most important thing I have learnt for creating long term relationships with potential customers, was being open and honest and using a few 'nudges' along the way.

I am sure we can all sell something short term, if we perhaps miss a few things out, give it away or leave an unanswered question, but it will come back on you or your reputation one day and, therefore, is not a way to grow a long term business. So be straight and be honest and, above all, listen – we have one mouth and two ears and we should use them in that ratio.

Note Things Down and Build a Rapport

I keep a note book that I write all my meetings in, write the names of people I meet and as I pick up snippets about their family, holidays and interests. Doing so helps me remember many of these things and it makes a huge difference in your relationship with your prospect or customer when you can ask a question or refer to something mentioned in the past. How many times have you been impressed with someone asking about a holiday or event that you may have mentioned a while ago?

This is not being cynical. It's about being interested in the person so that you can be sure that you deliver what they need. I am genuinely interested in people and I find the many hundreds of people that I deal with are quite fascinating once you dig below the surface. I would say that most people are very interesting if you get past the first stage. For instance, recently, I discovered after our second meeting, that one of my customers was the first person from his country to climb Mount Everest. By the third meeting, we had signed pictures and, given the seniority and formality of the first meeting, I would never have guessed that would happen. Everyone has a story somewhere; take time in your next meeting to see if you can find your customers.

Remember Names

I have several techniques. If I am in a presentation and there is a table or layout of people, I ask them to introduce themselves, while I create a picture in my notebook. Using the same actual positions the people are in I put their name and title or a quick note in each place.

Once I have that mental image in my mind, I can quickly recall a name or what they look like. How much better it is to call someone by name when replying to a point or question with a quick glance if required to your notes.

The second technique is to relate people to actors or objects and create that mental image in your mind as you look at them and get their name. So for my name, I would conjure up a tin with 'Mar; written on it and if I was in finance, a bunch of notes hovering over the tin, that image would sit above the persons head. For my wife Heather, I would see a bunch of the Heather plant with a vibrant purple flower. Complex to explain but easy to visualise!

Second names with large groups I have always found harder, but I can usually remember some of the easier ones and generally get the attendee list and fill in any gaps later and I know enough to place the person and what they looked like.

The third technique which works more with objects is to map them in your mind with rooms in my house. So the first object would be in your hallway, then to your left the next object would be in the dining room and to the right the third object would be in the lounge and so on until you run out of rooms or objects. This is a common memory technique and it works really well for me, allowing me to recall something for a number of days until I can get it written down.

Nudge Along Prospects

People are pretty good at making decisions, but in some situations, they are not. Sometimes you have to help them to get there as subtly as you can.

As I got older and a little wiser I realised that selling was like taking your customer down a long corridor with lots of exit doors. The objective was to close the doors before they got there, so in the end there was only one door left to take, even if it didn't always result in a sale. Indeed, if having qualified a prospect and then not sold to them, I took it as my fault rather than theirs, as somewhere along the line I left a door open or misunderstood or incorrectly qualified something.

I had the pleasure of working with one lady called Carolyn Bloor, who if you went out selling with her, you would find that her sales approach was the same with every visit. In fact she would go so far as to admit she was probably the most boring salesperson in the team. Yet she was by far the most successful in the history of the company. She was top salesperson seven years running, with the largest ever sale, best ever month, most product ever sold - all records that have never been beaten since. Her secret was no more than listening and gently guiding the customer down the corridor, using the same technique every time to ensure the exit doors were closed.

Use the Corridor-Selling Technique

First of all, you cannot sell someone something until you know what their requirement is (let's assume for this part of the book, they have a specific requirement). So the first thing you need to do is ask some open questions and listen, not just listen, but listen for the tiny clues that people give away in the way they talk, respond, sit and look.

Much of that comes with practice but most of us understand it intuitively. Don't assume you know what they want, even if the meeting is about a particular need. What we want to do is find their 'hot button' and earn their trust. Open questions include:

'I understand that you may be looking for X and it would help me to have a little more background information on your requirement.'
'We would welcome the chance to put forward a quote; can I just ask you a couple of questions to help me understand the requirement further?'

Within these questions you are looking to clarify a number of things: the timescale for decision; if a budget has been allocated; the process to decide the eventual supplier (if a shortlist is in place and who makes the final decision). If you cannot get this information, then it is really difficult to qualify this as a potential sale and determine how much time you should spend. Once you have the 'skittles' lined up of timescale, budget and sign off, you can start the journey down the sales corridor.

The next stage of the meeting is to reflect back some of the information you collected earlier, which confirms that you understand the requirement and at this point start looking for your 'edge'. What is it we can do or offer that shows our product or service is better than anything else they may be looking at. Is the prospect engaging with you, are they looking at you when they talk, does their body language feel right? If the answer is no, then before you can start down the sales corridor you need to perhaps ask further open questions, to see where the problem might lie. They could include the list below.

- Have they already made a decision, but are bringing you in to satisfy procurement?
- Do they really have a budget allocated?
- Is there a decision process and timescale?
- Or perhaps is the person just shy?

Only you can decide these things, but I know one thing for sure, that any doubts or unanswered questions are your open exit doors further down the corridor, so perhaps the sale may happen, but don't bet your future on it.

Once you feel you have all the information you require, then you can start the process of closing the sale. Bear in mind at this stage it could just be on a shortlist, a sale or a further presentation, but basically it gets you to the next stage.

In my business we would then move to demonstrating the product or service, using the information we gained earlier to ask qualifying questions as we progressed.

"You said you wanted some flexibility, from what I have shown you are you happy we can provide this?"

"You said reporting was important, does what I demonstrated meet with what you are looking for"

"From what I have shown you, are you happy with what we can offer?"

From here you need to revisit any points that raised questions and make sure they are happy that all the requirements outlined previously are satisfied. Now you have your first set of doors down the corridor closed. There are no major issues with the product or service against the requirement.

Next we have to run through pricing and again get an agreement that the pricing proposed is acceptable and within budget or signoff. You might say:

"You said you were happy with the product, if I am able to supply this within your budget, would you be happy with that?" Another set of doors closed.

Depending on the decision-making process, you may be able to close the sale at this point or at least ensure you are at the next stage. You have confirmed that they like your product, it is priced within budget and now you simply need to ask if they would place an order with you.

"Are you happy to proceed and place an order with me?"

At this point they cannot say you are too expensive or do not meet requirements, as we dealt with these points earlier. We would know if they had budget, what the sign off level is and the authority required as we asked this previously. If the answer is negative, then you have missed something in your presentation or meeting that left a door open somewhere.

This is a very simplistic approach and the real skill is listening for the clues and building trust and rapport, which takes practice. As I have mentioned many times, one of the best investments you will make is a good established sales course, which will put you ahead of the competition. The aim is to ensure that you are a nice person to do business with and that you understand those little 'nudges' that make the difference between selling and just having a good chat and going nowhere. Remember though that professional procurement people go on similar courses, so they will tell you everything is over budget, there is no money, that decisions take ages, but in the end it's all a negotiation to get the best product for the best price.

Selling Internationally

When we sold our first product outside the UK, it was quite exciting and of course the next thought was how much more could we sell? What we learnt along the way was that there are some considerations you need to take into account.

Example

Our first foray into international markets was a bit of a disaster. Looking back on what we did, we could see a number of mistakes so we learnt the hard way what worked and what didn't work for our products. These lessons are generic to whatever you decide to do.

We had got it into our head that there was a huge market in the USA for our products and having sold a few over the phone from web enquiries, it seemed a natural expansion to modify what we had for the USA marketplace. Most of the work was changing any references to currency and changing spelling and we created some new artwork to pull it all together.

The first trip was to be an exhibitor at a major trade fair and armed with brochures, business cards and products we flew over for the first time to the Gaylord Opryland Convention Center in Nashville. That in itself was an experience, with 2881 rooms, its own indoor river and boat ferry it is more like a small city than a hotel and there we were, a couple of pull up stands, some demonstration products and a box full of brochures.

It didn't help that I was exhausted. Tom, who I travelled with was claustrophobic, so within 10 minutes of getting on the plane, he wanted to get off and we ended up swapping around seats, so he could have a window seat and I was left stuck between two rather large men for the best part of eight hours.

Well, once we got used to the difference in style that American shows had over the U shows, where we had a booth instead of a stand and a curtain instead of a backdrop, it all seemed as we expected; although I certainly wasn't prepared for how friendly the Americans were.

Over the three days we were there, most people who were registered attendees came to our stand to see what we were selling and over the three days we amassed well over a hundred potential leads. We clapped our hands together in joy, packed our bags and came home.

And that's when reality struck. Once we came home, I prioritised the leads into a, b and c *(a - urgent, c - when you have cleared the others and b - somewhere between)*. I picked the phone up and started calling and came across one of the big differences between Europe and the USA - voice mail. So I emailed those I couldn't speak to and worked around the time difference. It was pointless. Apart from a small licence we sold to a European company based in the USA, we sold nothing.

Now I think I am ok at selling and I did try, to the extent that I visited the USA another three or four times, making meetings from the show and finding other companies to visit, but really we never ever got any traction.

That brought home the first lesson I learnt in international selling, as soon as you go home, all the doors close behind you. Local people want to deal with local people. The whole exercise in the USA cost us the best part of six figures in investment and lost opportunity, but we came away with a valuable lesson that helped us in the future: if you want to sell local then be local. Even if it's a partner, distributor, serviced office or agent, you need to have someone on the ground if you want to be taken seriously long term.

Before you go away with the idea that international selling is too big a risk let me assure you that you can succeed. We did. It was a question of approaching everything the right way and sometimes getting a helping hand when you need.

Government Help

There are grants and funds in UK the that can help you with overseas expansion and although these have been cut back in the last couple of years, there is still 'matched' funding of around £5000 available. Be aware though, that the situation is in flux like the economy, so check what is available at the time you read this.

In the UK, one of the Schemes is 'Passport to Export', a UK Government scheme that aims to encourage export. You sign up for around a £150 and in return you get some training, access to experts, invitations to UK sponsored events and to join subsidized trade missions. You also get (as of the time of writing this) £500 towards an international flight and a further £1500 towards marketing activities, such as shows and access to further funding. Given that it is free, it really is a no-brainer.

When we explored Australia and the Middle East we took advantage of the schemes and attended a trade mission to Dubai and Abu Dhabi and the contacts we were introduced to helped us immensely. In Australia, the UK Trade and Industry Office (UKTI), through their Australian counterparts, arranged office space, seminar rooms and access to resources to help us understand the employment laws and visa regulations. I would go so far as to say that the help they gave us enabled us to move quicker than we could have under our own devices and everyone wants to help you succeed.

In the UK, there is a programme called OMIS, which stands for Overseas Market Introduction Service, and is run through the local British Embassy in the country you wish to work in. The cost can be anything from £1000 to £2500 depending on what you want out of it, but in essence the local embassy will do everything to arranging meetings with key clients, to holding a reception for you in the Embassy. It depends on your business, but it worked really well for me.

We set up from scratch an office in Australia and so the help we got from the local UKTI office allowed us to make sure we stayed legal. Operating initially as a branch office that could price in Australian dollars but had to process in English pounds (yes it was a nightmare) we quickly moved to a fully operational Australian PTY company, with local bank account.

Taking one of our top UK people and sending them out to run the Australian office was a gamble, but it paid off handsomely. The style of selling in the UK is more direct and fast than many Australian companies, so we very quickly established a presence and within a month it became clear we needed a second person and an office (rather than a virtual office which we had initially).

This office grew very fast and we found that the focused selling that we used in the UK, clear packages and timely follow up helped tremendously.

Cold Calling and Lead Generation

Cold calling can leave some people in a cold sweat, but really it's all a question of using the right approach so that you can get the substantial rewards that it can bring. The techniques you use can depend on your market: is it local, particularly relevant if you are in a retail environment, is it postcode based, regional or international?

My experience has primarily been regional and international. Within our training business very few people purchased locally, so most of our campaigns were focused across the UK or abroad.

When we started out, all we had was a single product, a telephone and some market knowledge. So over the years we developed a pattern of working that all new people to the business would go through to develop business in their geography. I will cover that in a bit more detail.

Having worked with a large number of businesses, I am still amazed by the number of owners, who knowing more about the market and their product than anyone else, still do not want to pick up the phone and call.

I do realise it may seem hard and you may think this area belongs to some special breed of sales professional, but honestly you are often the best sales person for your area or company. So let's run through some basics of selling and where to get started.

Getting Set Up to Cold Call

First you need to make sure you have everything that you require to satisfy any enquiry or appointment. So you need a brochure or brochures (electronic and paper preferably), a website, a good email address, business cards and some standard letters that you can edit with details on the products, services and pricing (if applicable).

Paula's Top Tips

In all my time in selling, finding exceptional telemarketing people who can cold call is a challenge, and one of the best I have worked with for the volume of successful calls that lead to sales is Paula Gower. Paula has a system that works and I asked her to let me have some hints and tips for anyone starting out cold calling from a telephone.

For Paula no one day is the same and from the comfort of her office chair she gets to speak to people all over the world and build up relationships just from listening and talking. She would say that the greatest buzz ever is to make that one call to a key person, confirm that great appointment and to have the sales person close a large sale for the benefit of everyone.

If you are telemarketing or cold calling for the first time, Paula has some tips for you to think about and we have listed them below.

Be polite. At all times, show empathy, always appreciate that you are interrupting someone's day but never apologise for it! It's a fine line but just be polite and sound polite. A receptionist will always remember either a very polite lady from ABC products or the very rude one! Receptionists are sometimes the key to getting through to high level contacts, and it is important to always make the right impression.

Be in a good place. Before you pick up the phone, put yourself physically and mentally, in a good place. Make your working surroundings calm and well organised, be comfortable, if you are physically calm and at ease this will come through in your voice. Have around you pictures of things that are your goals and aims and put in place your own incentives. For example photos of that car you are striving for, a picture of the hotel you've always wanted to stay in.

Start early. Always start the day early and organised, it sounds easy, but if you don't do this, the stress will become apparent in your voice.

Know what you're selling. Learn your product, and understand how you can create an interest, pick out key elements and be passionate about them.

Keep it simple. When you first start out, you may think everyone else is listening (which they are) but as this book teaches, keep it simple.

Practise to be perfect. Practise as much as you need to; even go as far as recording yourself, you will be taken aback how many little mannerisms you have, that you were not aware of.

Get on your feet. Stand up, you will be surprised how much better you can project yourself if you stand up when calling, and that confidence will come across in your voice.

Start the day right. Start your day with a good call, find a team member or a friend to call that will put you in a good place, clear any frogs in the throat, smile and off you go to your first call.

Enjoy the positives. Celebrate the good call, give out a cheer, there is no greater buzz than getting the appointment or result that you want – share it with your colleagues, smile, and keep that feeling in your head.

Learn from the negatives. If it goes wrong, and you have a bad call then acknowledge it, learn from it and move on. If you need to take a break and get a drink, and reflect on what went wrong, that's fine, but never ever dwell on it. Remember this is about people, and other people can have bad days as well. I can now handle most objections over the phone, but that skill came from many bad calls as well as good calls.

Use your organisational skills. Be organised and confirm any appointment or action by email to the customer straight away, if it is a meeting be clear when, where and who is going to be there.

Note System and Follow-Up

You also want a system to record calls and follow ups – if you have not done this before, then just create a paper based system where you can print out a handful of contact sheets and keep in a folder. Simple headings such as date called, who, company, telephone number, details and follow up action is a good start. You can use a spread sheet, whatever you feel comfortable with, but just be consistent and remember to back things up and to transfer everything if you move to a new system. Over time, this will become your goldmine for information and follow ups.

Finding Prospects

Next you need people to call. They fall into two categories: those that have a requirement and you are perhaps selling against the incumbent supplier; those that are just simply a cold call to introduce yourselves and your service.

Perhaps in your market these are much the same, for example if your target market is the NHS, it becomes much easier to drill down to who you are going to call and what you are going to say.

If you have any head start, such as you already have customers in say the Fire Service, then concentrate on calling all the other Fire Services around the country, before you start on a new market. You may have mailed them and got no response, but nothing beats a good phone call.

If your market is geographic then I would start with regional business magazines, which contain names and contact within companies that you can call. Our local magazine lists the top 50 companies in the area; the Sunday Times lists the top 200 companies in the UK.

You also have trade directories. Binleys do a directory of local authorities, NHS, Fire, Police and Ambulance, with contacts and phone numbers. The training managers' yearbook contains details of most large companies in the UK with the HR and training contacts. If you do your research there will be a trade directory that contains contacts for your industry – or if you have a generic product or service, then look for directories that list the type of buyer you are looking for.

The other great area to find information is Google. I worked for a while in the project management area and I would Google 'project manager minutes' and 'project manager agenda' – of course you would get a zillion hits, but you need to narrow your search down to the UK, change the date range to be in the last year and then go to the end of the listings and work back.

That may sound odd, but while most of the front third of pages will find competitors and products you are not interested in, filed away at the back Google has indexed publicly available information from company meetings where 'project management' is on an agenda or mentioned in the minutes of a meeting. If you want to be geographic then add a location to the search to narrow it down further. You will be surprised how many quangos, departments and companies you have never heard of appear. Because of our instant-on world, paper directories can be a year out of date, but a Google entry can be just weeks old. This has worked really well for me, but as you can see from the search term I used, you have to be able to define what you are looking for into a couple of words.

LinkedIn, as mentioned earlier is also a great way to prospect, however as it becomes more popular it is getting harder to be unique, but as a way of researching a company and its staff I think it works really well.

Also the 'Groups' function allows you to join a group that is relevant to you and of course you can see other members, which you could invite to link with you. Sales messages are frowned on in LinkedIn, so keep communication at a technical level and show people your knowledge leadership.

You also will have local support usually through your Chamber of Commerce, which you can join and they will help you find business contacts and most local authorities have someone who looks after developing local business. Once you have someone to phone, if you are new to this, then we need to get some flow in what you say.

What to Say

Although I am giving a high level overview, if you are new to selling, it's really important you get this right. You can have the best product in the world but if no-one knows about it, then you are doomed to fail or stay second best. Put yourself on a basic two day sales course, covering calling, sales cycles and closing, it will be the best thing you have invested in – yourself!

I like role play – so I get someone to pretend to be a buyer (usually my long-suffering wife) and we figure out a scenario and what some of the objections could be. You will be surprised how it will help, as they say practice makes perfect.

The important part of your call is what you say and how you open. There are lots of barriers to you getting through to the person you want and it also depends if the person you want is cold called all day long by other companies.

As a tip, try to find the path of least resistance. So as an example, a typical buyer for me would be a training manager or HR person. Now everyone and their dog calls them day in and day out, so it's going to be tough, so I change my calling and concentrate on the 'recommender', the person that hopefully recommends to the training department to use my company. In my case it would be a project manager or project director – if I get it right and they like me and my products, they will become my 'inside' salesperson and clear the path through the training department.

It's the same with Information Technology, you are never going to have great success getting hold of the IT manager or director of a large company, but if you are selling software or services, then perhaps the Help Desk or Development team would be a good place to start. Have a think about who your recommenders would be. So we have a contact and we are now refining our message. Some tips on what I think have worked well and is pretty simple.

Busy people are busy people and calling is a bit like gambling, you are hoping that you get the right person who at that time has a requirement for your product or service. We have all been there, you get called regularly by people offering a service that you don't want, but then one day you need that service, no one calls, but you do remember the one guy that was nice and sent information, which you probably filed somewhere– you call him back or find him on the Internet. You are more likely to give that person the opportunity than anyone else. So persevere with your calling and always follow up, there may be no requirement today, but that doesn't mean there won't be one tomorrow.

One thing you will find is that usually there is a 'gatekeeper' – a term we use for someone that you need to get through to get to the person you want. Remember they are only doing their job. You do not have to convince them about your product, but why they should put YOU through. Be polite, show empathy, ask for their help, and if you agree a time to call back, stick to it.

Keep your call simple, please don't ask them 'how they are' - it's a classic sales pitch and you really don't care at this point anyway, so why ask? Why would a complete stranger who is very busy open up a conversation about their health? Much better to get to the point of what you have to offer and enquire if that is something they are looking at or perhaps will in the future. A good example of what I use is:

"Good morning, my name is MK from ABC, we have launched a great product in the area of XYX, which we believe is market leader"

"Can I take a couple of minutes to show you what we have and if it is of interest, we can take it further, if not then at least you have seen what is available.

Then wait … silence used reasonably often gets the other person to respond and you will get their answer. If the response is they are not interested then pose a couple of other quick close questions before you end the conversation:

"Are you likely to be looking at this area at some stage in the future? Would you mind if I called back in 3 months?"

"Is there someone else in the organisation that would look after this area, would you mind if I got their contact details to send some information to?"

There are a hundred different ways the conversation can go, but the rule is 'listen, listen, listen' look for clues in what they say, how they talk to you, if they are rushed, do they seem open to talk further etc., all these things you will get more experienced at the more you do it.

The other thing to avoid where possible is going into too much detail over the phone, what may sound fascinating to you may be pretty boring to them and they may just be too polite to say with the result that you think you are having a good conversation, when you are not. If you are talking longer on the phone, drop in questions to check where you are, such as:

"What do you currently use in that area?"

"How many people do you think this would be applicable to" or whatever the questions would be for your product or service.

Generally try to avoid questions that have a 'yes' or 'no' answer, otherwise it starts to get like a quiz show, the challenge is to get them talking, so they engage with you and you then start to build rapport.

I have found in my selling career that honesty works well and this was particularly so when we were starting out and if you can get it right, people will want to help you, particularly if you are local to them. I would open by introducing myself and saying that we were a new local company with some great products, looking to get established and wondered if we could run through what we have for sale. That worked well for us in the early days. As I mentioned earlier you should invest in a selling course, if you are new to this area, it will make a huge difference particularly when it comes to closing sales.

Tenacity is a great trait and you will need lots of it – just keep calling, set aside time where you start at say 8am and go through to 11am and then take a break and again from 3pm to 6pm. Don't look at emails, get distracted or anything else, think of yourself as a robot, as soon as you put down the phone, pick it up for the next call, try and automate the calling routine and keep focused and positive. Your best calls will probably be before 9am and after 5pm, when people are less busy and secretaries have gone home. If you are going to leave voice mail messages, try and leave them at the end of the day, so that they are the first thing the person picks up in the morning.

Once you have some calling sessions under your belt, you can start to review the calls, the success rate, the responses and potential opportunities. If it's not working then tweak it, role play it through with a colleague and try again. What works for you may be different to everyone else. I have never been a fan of recording calls, but you can record and the listen to yourself and how you talk and what you say.

Follow up is very important, if you promise something, make sure you deliver it and that allows you to do another follow up as a next step.

At this stage you may be asking yourself why bother when you could hire telemarketing agencies who would do all this for you at the early stages but unless you have tried it yourself, how can you tell someone else how to do it? Once you're established and business grows, you can then take on further sales people and hopefully even dedicated telemarketing resource with the benefit of knowing that you have led from the front. This way no one call pull the wool over your eyes and you can spot non-performers regardless of their excuses and deal with them quickly.

Trust me when I say you will get it wrong sometimes, but don't beat yourself up about it; just focus on the next opportunity. I have sat in sales where I have quoted a price and the decision has been so instant, I realised I may have under quoted and could have made a better deal. Equally I gambled wrong and lost a sale because I miss-read the situation. The best you can do is learn from it and not make the same mistake again as I did.

Example 1

One of my very first appointments, the horror I can still recall vividly even now, was a cold call to a major wholesaler, who said yes, they are interested and could I come over and meet. The contact was a director and I put the phone down in a cold sweat, my first major appointment with a top decision maker in a household name company.

I packed up my case, laptop, brochures, new tie, smart suit and off I went. I got lost on the way (no sat nav or Google maps back then), and arrived a couple of minutes late and of course I am now panicking. Found reception, a smart new building in Swindon and presented myself and signed in. I was desperate to use the loo and when I put the tap on to wash my hands, I put it on full and it splashed out down the front of my jacket and trousers and left me with a dark mark on the front of my jacket.

I signed in at reception, put my case down and got my badge, completely forgot about my case and promptly turned around and tripped over it. Finally I sat in reception and Mr X, came over and introduced himself and it was one of those times I caught my handshake wrong and he ended up squeezing the ends of my fingers together, not a great start.

I did my best to pick things up as we went up the single flight of stairs, but it was not meant to be and I didn't pick up my feet enough and tripped forward on the stairs narrowly missing Mr X with my briefcase. We made his office with not much else going wrong and he got me a coffee and you have to picture me sitting opposite him, on a round table. I made notes, chatted about what we did and as I am listening to him I started to play with the spring clip badge they gave me on my pocket and all I can remember is the badge pinging (that's the best way I can describe it) up in the air and in slow motion towards Mr X's head, in my horror, I swung my hand to try and catch it caught my coffee cup and sent it flying. We sat in silence for a couple of seconds, the coffee over the table and over my notes, the badge on the floor and he said 'you're not having a good day are you – shall we wind up and call it a day?' and that's exactly what I did and I couldn't get out fast enough.

Example 2

The other quick story I will tell you is about a good presentation I had many years ago with a new customer (that one went well) and I proudly used my new Toshiba laptop that at today's prices would be classed expensive. All went well except the md was flying back from Manchester to London and as I was going that way I offered to take him to the airport.

I put my laptop down by my door and went round to open his door for him and then jumped in myself and reversed out of the parking space. I hit the kerb lightly so went back in and came out again at a better angle, when it dawned on me, it wasn't the kerb; it was my laptop.

I calmly opened the door and there, laying on the floor, was a laptop bag with tyre marks across it. Oh my God – that's the first laptop we had been able to afford, my wife is going to kill me. I stepped out picked it up and put it in through the back door. Mr MD who was reading some notes was oblivious of what had happened and we went off to Manchester airport as if nothing had happened.

I dropped him off, found a quiet spot and then went into panic mode, what had I done? And there was no happy ending, the car had destroyed the screen and made the laptop about an inch less in thickness than before and I lost everything. But the customer was no wiser and we got the business over time. My wife was mad at me, but we got over it and saved enough to replace the laptop again.

What I am trying to say is that nothing is perfect, there is no magic other than your own, but by trying and trying you will get things

170

happen that normal people in normal jobs may never experience, but you will succeed trust me.

Setting Sales Targets

Most people have an idea of what they want to achieve in their business, but I am still amazed by the number of businesses that I deal with that do not have specific targets. There is usually a budget in place, but rarely that vital element, the communication of what exactly that means to each person in the business.

Put simply, I take my business plan, work out what I need to earn to cover my overheads each month, averaging it out and ironing out any bumps, and then double it. So let's say that we have a cost base of £25,000 a month including all expenditure, base salaries (don't worry too much about commission and bonus payments related to sales). I would suggest for most businesses (and it may vary depending what you are selling) you should double that to £50,000 to make a good starting point to allocate as your monthly target.

Then you need to work out who is responsible for selling, which would include yourself and any members of your team that sell, and divide the target down between them. I usually add another 10% as well, so that there is a little bit of a buffer.

Remember that you have to be reasonable about what you think each person can achieve: if the target is too high it becomes demotivating; if the target is too low it is no longer a challenge. Only you can work out what you think is the right balance.

In my business, I generally think a good salesperson can generate around £25,000 of profit, so given my target that means I would have two people selling, which could include me. I would give each person a target of £27,500, and build a commission scheme around that amount.

Once you have a target you need to communicate that clearly and break it down into monthly and quarterly as well. Now that we have a target, we need to build a package around it to motivate the team to meet and hopefully exceed it. This is another area that many businesses make complex and although I can understand why it might be so in some cases, I find that my favourite saying "if you can't draw it with a crayon you can't sell it" applies to commission as well.

In an ideal world when a salesperson sells something, at that point they should be able to work out what it means to them in terms of commission. If the scheme is too complex, then the chances are that your salesperson will not know where they are in terms of commission due and that may affect the final push at the end of a quarter or month.

So let's take our target of £27,500, give a single rate of commission up to the target, a nice monthly bonus if they achieve it, and then a higher rate of commission for sales above that point. Finally add a bonus for meeting the quarter target, and finally the annual target. Nice and simple!

Generally in running our sales teams I based my forecast on a good salesperson meeting 8 out of 12 monthly bonus payments, and 3 out of 4 quarter payments, plus the annual bonus payment. Quite often someone could only get one monthly bonus, but still get a quarter bonus because they did well over target one month but were under target for two months.

Make sure you have a regular sales meeting, a minimum of once a month, and use tools such as Skype, if you have a remote based team. Be honest and open on where you are in terms of sales, as any underperformance is everyone's problem, not just yours.

Typically, we would review the previous month's performance against targets, look ahead for the current month, and for the next three months. Prospects would be labelled A, B and C. This was so that I knew that any 'A' prospect had ticked all the boxes and we were just waiting for a purchase order; that a 'B' would be potential to close but perhaps we were on a shortlist; that 'C' were rank outsiders but that given the right opportunity would close this month.

Your experience of the business and asking the right questions will help you understand if the prospects had been qualified correctly and how confident you could be that the revenue discussed for that month was going to happen.

No matter what business you have - be it a retail shop or a manufacturing company - make sure you have clear targets that everyone understands and communicate them on a regular basis.

A final note about sales meetings, I always involved the whole company so everyone felt part of the challenge and some of the best ideas came from the most surprising people. In larger companies perhaps involve the whole section or department and make sure you have good representation from other departments that help out. It's all about team work.

Customer Service

One of the products we developed was online training, so whilst there were huge development costs, when we sold something it was all profit and 100% of it stayed in our pockets. If you have this luxury, then my first piece of advice is if you have a disagreeable customer, then just give them a refund, it's not worth the hassle that unhappy customers can create in this instant-on world we live in.

Complaints

We used to offer a seven-day guarantee and no one ever came back, but we did have a couple of telephone complaints, both a couple of months into the licence. Both people came armed with a hundred reasons why the course was not right for them and both were taken aback when we just agreed to give them a complete refund. It's the only time I have ever got a positive review from someone who started out wanting a fight!

I often use TripAdvisor for my travels and I do accept, like many people, that there will always be someone that doesn't like something, no matter how good. So I take an average of the reviews and as long as (using Pareto's Law) around 80% were good then I am happy with that. However what really made me confident was the hotels that had personally responded to any complaint and made an effort to find out more or explain what happened. And there's the thing: don't hide from complaints. The best we can ever achieve in this world is to please most of the people most of the time, certainly trying to make all the people happy all of the time, is a tough task when you have a bigger business. So next time someone complains, whether in person or electronically make the effort to be as reasonable as you can to try to sort the problem.

Example

A customer referred me to a forum, where an American user had been very critical of our handling of his purchase and subsequent follow up nearly a year before. This was coming up in the search engines when you searched on our company.

I registered on the forum and emailed the person for his details, there was no response, so I got in touch with the moderators of the forum, explaining that we were not aware of the complaint and wanted to address it. They prompted the user who gave me his telephone details and on talking to him indeed the service we offered had not been up to scratch.

I offered an unconditional refund on the basis they updated their comments with what we had agreed. They got their money back and the bad comment disappeared off the forum. That was worth a lot to me just to clear the negative comments from the search engines and it worked.

Body Language

To round things off, I thought it may be worth exploring a few hints and tips about body language. Many people that work for me, know it's one of my 'things' that I look for and I really believe it helps you spot non-verbal communication that could affect your opportunity.

There is a great book called 'Body Language' by Allan Pease, which I purchased back in 1985 and which now comes in an updated form "The Definitive Book of Body Language". It doesn't matter whether you go for the new or old for they're both useful and, despite its age, the old one even today is one of the best reference guides to reading people through their gestures.

In a meeting, for example, someone may well be agreeing with me, but the non-verbal body language can tell me if something is at odds with what they are saying. It's not a perfect science but as in Pareto's Law, understanding just 20% of what to look for, can make a difference.

Most body language is pretty common throughout the world, such as smiling, frowning, shaking the head for no or yes and some of this is inborn and others learned.

Wherever you are and whoever you are with, one of Allan Pease's points is worth remembering: do not interpret a solitary gesture without looking for supporting gestures, otherwise a tickly nose with a cold, could be mistaken for something else! With that in mind here are a few tell-tale signs to look out for.

Clenched hands can sometimes be taken as negative. If I am dealing with someone that has clenched hands in front of them, even if they are smiling, to me it would suggest they are holding something back, and it may require a few more open questions to decide if I have missed something.

If my customer has his hand over his mouth, or touching his nose or rubbing his eye, again I would look to see if I have missed something, as these can indicate a negative attitude.

I also look for crossed arms, generally this can be a defensive or negative response, and often by stepping back to previous questions and asking open questions, you can see the arms unfold and the person relax.

It's often the same with crossed legs, although many people like me just find that comfortable, but if I see it with folded arms, then I take it as I am not on target with whatever I am proposing.

If we are standing, and the other person crosses their legs, then I become aware that they may have some negative thoughts, and again by open questions, you can often see them uncross their legs and relax.
Something else that can feel weird, but works, is to copy the other person's gestures, such as leaning forward, or hands behind the head. You will be surprised how often you do this without thinking, and it can help to gain acceptance.

The only other major thing I look for, particularly when in groups, is the way people stand, and where their feet point. Next time you are at a party, look at where people point their feet, or at least one of them. Subconsciously, people point their feet (or foot) towards a place to which they wish to go or to a person with whom they wish to become more involved.

People rarely face each other unless it is more intimate; mostly they create a triangular zone, and if you are joining a group you look for them to move their feet so at least one foot is pointed to you, that would signal acceptance in the group. If they keep their feet pointing away from you, then you can take it you are not so welcome and you may be interrupting something. I find that rule works well where I have to socialise with a group of people, as part of a business function.

The other part of 'body language' I think works well is the positioning of the people in the meeting. I do try, as much as I can, never to have a meeting either at the side of a desk or table. It is not always possible but the desk creates a competitive defensive position, where the desk becomes the territory. Sounds far-fetched, I know, but think about areas like a doctor's surgery. Traditionally we met the doctor with a desk between us; now the doctor will sit and face us, making us feel more relaxed.

If you have the opportunity to decide where to sit, then always try and sit on the same side as your customer, in something like a boardroom, or on the corner of the table so you can sit next to them.

I will prepare meeting rooms to make my customers feel at ease. So I plan where they are to sit or if I am in the conference room early I will pick a corner position to be next to the person I want to meet with.

You can spend a lot of time on learning these things, but just enough knowledge will give you the edge over your competitors, and that's all you need.

Martyn's Top Tips

- Be honest and open.
- Make sure you follow a step-by-step method to selling.
- Use the corridor technique.
- Be brave.
- Agree targets.
- Keep customers happy.
- Watch the body language.

References and Resources

UKTI: http://www.ukti.gov.uk/home.html?guid=none.
OMIS:
http://www.ukti.gov.uk/export/howwehelp/overseasmarketintrod
uctionservice.html.
Passport to Export:
http://www.ukti.gov.uk/export/howwehelp/passporttoexport.html
.

The Definitive Book of Body Language, Allan Pease and Barbara Pease.

CULTIVATE AND COMPETE

Step 9

"The basis of our partnership strategy and our partnership approach: We build the social technology. They provide the music." ~ Mark Zuckerberg

There are many ways to give your business the 'edge' that I have been talking about. Here, I look at some ways you can cultivate and work with other organisations in order to compete.

Partners and Distributors

My experience in working with partners and resellers is based around using third parties to deliver products and services into markets that we could cover directly. Joint ventures, agencies, distributors and partners are many variations of almost the same thing and without them many businesses would be unable to develop and flourish. That said, I have a couple of words of caution, particularly if you are a fairly new business looking to expand, about the pitfalls I have found using this route.

Example

On the whole I sold direct to end users, but as we developed, we started looking at partnerships as a way to achieve this. The UK market leader in our industry who we always looked up to and aspired to be was a company we can call 'P'. Although we were relative newcomers we were making headway. Our product was fairly unique in that it provided online training whilst every other competitor we knew of provided classroom based training. Business was growing well to the extent that we were, pretty much doubling in size every year. We obviously caught P's eye. Through contacts P expressed an interest in distributing our products and we were very excited, as it could have accelerate our business further into new major accounts.

Agreements were put in place and demonstrations and product material provided, meetings took place with the sales teams and I personally spent weeks working on joint tenders to some of the biggest government departments in the UK.

And then we waited for the orders to come in. And we waited, and we waited. But nothing seemed to be actually clicking.

It took a while for the penny to drop, but it did. It was after finding a copy of some bids that P won, but where the customer decided not to take our products as part of the solution, that I finally figured it out.

What P was doing was 'ticking the box'. So a major proposal would include an option for online training, but when you looked at the pricing the online option looked more expensive than the classroom option. They were using the online training to promote the classroom as better and more cost effective. This whole exercise cost us time and effort and delayed us by keeping us out of the market for a period.

I guess it was obvious really - their sales teams were commissioned on classroom training, the business model was built on classroom training, why would they want to bring in another product that would compete with that. However, by having it on the price list they could show they offered a comprehensive solution, even if they never sold it.

This became one of my major rules as we expanded the business, whoever you work with, if they sell their own products as well as yours, no matter how complimentary they are, they will always give priority to their own products and while they may use your products as a lever it will only be to open doors for them not for yours.

So be careful when you look at partnering with someone, make sure they are not going to slow you down or trip you up. We did appoint partners internationally and this is the basis for my second word of caution.

Our initial partner in Australia used to sell a reasonable amount of training for us, but was very slow. When the contract came up for renewal we tried an experiment. We sent two people over to Australia on a plane with a bunch of products and, backed by marketing help from the local UK Trade and Industry office, we ran free seminars across five major cities.

Well the results were amazing. The two people took more money in sales in two weeks than we had sold in a year through the partner. That was the catalyst for opening the Sydney office, which has gone from strength to strength since that time and become the second biggest market outside the UK.

Professional Bodies

Are you a member of any trade associations or professional bodies within your industry? In most industries there is a recognized association that you can join and over the years I have learnt that in many cases there are more benefits to joining than not.

Generally there are two types of bodies you want to join, those in your industry and those that are in the industry you want to sell to – which may not always be the same one.

For those that are in your industry you usually get to attend events with similar companies to yourself, be it a trade show or a workshop and sometimes using the accreditation logo on your paperwork can make a difference to how your potential prospects see you.

Usually there is a trade magazine, a members' magazine, plus other fringe benefits at a normally reasonable cost. I figured out that associations were a good way to find customers to drum up more business and find a way into new markets, as you are always doing in sales. It was fairly simple.

Example

We started by joining a whole range of professional bodies in our target market. We got sent through a handbook of other members, contacts, telephone and email addresses, a magazine we could advertise in and invitations to special events.

Of course we used the list 'gently' so as not to get into trouble but it really worked well for us and with one particular association, we made a lot of revenue from its members just by a gentle sales call explaining what we did.

It is worth saying, that the pitch we made was tailored to the people we were calling, specific to that industry and where we could we could show other customers in the same area.

We also ran a regular little advert in the magazine which started to get our name around and, since it wasn't a mainstream publication, advertising rates were much cheaper. We would get an entry in the members' directory and depending on the industry we would attend some of the regional meetings just to get to meet people.

Accreditation

Credibility and trust are cornerstones of business and accreditation can help you get that. One of the lessons I have learnt along the way is that accreditation is important, not only to you, but the potential customer you are selling to.

We're back to the principle I described at the beginning of the book where the customer is the most important part of the business equation.

What drives the customer to want the product or service? Why does the prospect want your product or service? If they are learning something, it will probably be important to them personally in their career development or for their next job. If it's a learning product perhaps it is required to meet criteria to reach accreditation.

Most companies have ISO9001 certification, a recognized worldwide standard showing that a company has been audited for quality and sends out a message that it is a professional to deal with. In fact some companies will not deal with suppliers who do not have ISO9001, so there is a motivation to achieve it.

Now within the ISO9001 industry, there are people who provide training, both to end users (what is involved in going through certification and how to prepare for it) and the very consultants who do the audits. There are tools - both paper and computer based - you can buy to help you and spin offs-in every direction to associations and discussion groups.

The motivation of the company who wants ISO9001 certification is to be recognized by their suppliers and get on the procurement lists where this certification is mandatory. So they have a requirement we can sell to and once we understand how, then we can replicate the same sales process to all potential companies seeking this certification.

So by finding the driver for a particular market or type of company, we can focus down and create a specific campaign around that. Unless you can find these drivers, such as the ISO certification, then it is a lot harder to not only find the right people, but for them to have the motivation to purchase from you at that time.

Martyn's Top Tips

- If you partner with someone who sells a similar product or is in your market beware.
- Join professional bodies to become a thought leader.
- Get accredited to boost your credibility.

References and Resources

ISO: http://www.iso.org/iso/home.html.

STEP 10

AVOID THE CREDIT CRUNCH

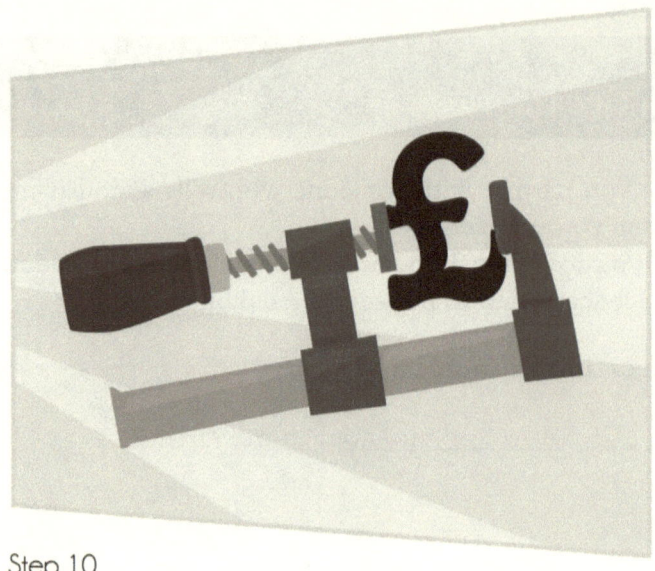

Step 10

"Remember that credit is money." ~ Benjamin Franklin

I have been extremely fortunate to have my wife Heather as my credit controller; she keeps an eye on everything coming in and everything going out and is probably one of the best credit controllers on the planet! In all the years of business we have only had one bad debt, which we just didn't see coming, but generally the majority of cash owing is collected within 30 days and very rarely gets over 45 days unless we have pre-agreed it.

I thought it worth putting this section in, as most business people in my experience are not that great at collecting money.

Record Spending and Invoicing

To confirm some basics first, whatever business you are in, you must have some way of keeping a record of what you spend and what you invoice. Doesn't matter if it is a paper system or a computerised system - at any one point you should be able to find out how much you owe, how much is owed to you, what is overdue and if necessary if you are below or above budget.

Budget to Avoid Overspending

So we have a budget and Heather reminds me on a regular basis to update it as required, so we can spot any overspend before it becomes an issue or drop in revenues. Without this basic information you are in huge danger if things go wrong of finding yourself on the edge of a cliff looking down and we have done this, so I can talk from experience.

We developed a simple pattern with Heather's job being to consider our finances, and my job every month would to focus on the revenue figure required, so Heather would tell me how much I needed to get in to cover costs and make a profit and that became my sole focus.

Collect Payments Due

Then of course you have to collect the money and Heather developed a system that worked really well, getting the majority owed into the bank in under 30 days.

Follow Up Invoices

After I sold the account, Heather would call them, sometimes before raising the invoice and ensure that all the details were correct for the right person and right office. Then, after it was sent, she would give them a call usually 10 days into the debt to check they had it in their system and that there were no issues. If for any reason there was a problem, it was sorted out there and then. About 23-25 days after the invoice was issued, Heather would ring again and check there were no problems in us receiving payment on the due date. Usually by now Heather had a contact name and had started to build some rapport. At this point if there was going to be a delay or something was wrong generally, it would be identified. The majority of invoices from this point were paid on time.

Sometimes customers will delay payment, but as long as you are prepared for it, then you can manage it. Sounds simple but most business struggle with good credit control and it is as important as selling the product, to ensure you are paid for it in a timely manner and that you don't sit around waiting for payment, only to be told that they have no record of the invoice or it went to the wrong person.

Martyn's Top Tips

- Develop a system.
- Stick to the system.
- Communicate with your customers.

STEP 11

NEW PRODUCT DEVELOPMENT

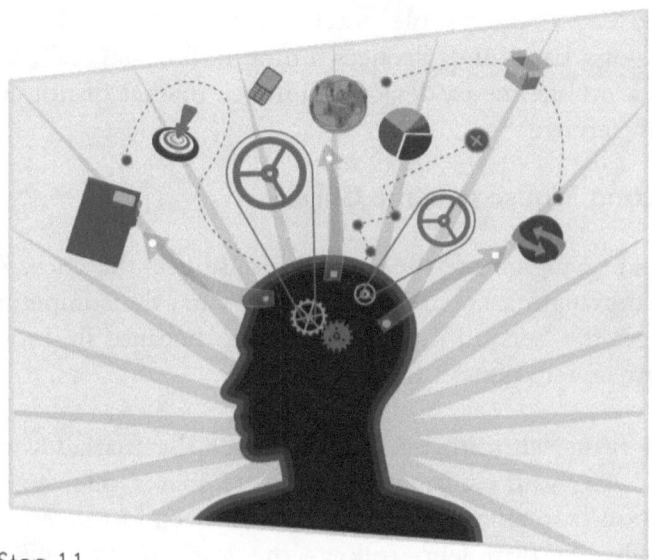

Step 11

"The early bird gets the worm but the second mouse gets the cheese." ~ Unknown

New product or service development is important for every organisation. Mobile is also a key part of business and is the direction the world is going. Both offer opportunities so it's understandably tempting to get over excited about a product or jump on the mobile bandwagon; however, I learnt a valuable lesson that should make us all cautious about both.

We took some of our educational information and developed a game that could run on a mobile phone, alongside short video clips of the materials.

We launched this with a bit of a fan fair, it being the first mobile media game of its kind in our market, and the response was great, we got magazine interviews and even made Sky TV about how we were successfully using apps in education. So lots of column inches and air time later, how did we do?

Well, not so good. When it came down to it most of our market preferred the old fashioned way of using the internet and good old fashioned CDs. Sure people purchased the apps we developed but we only got a handful of licences a month. No one really wanted to learn on a mobile media device within our market or not enough to make a difference.

The Second Mouse gets the Cheese

As the old saying goes: "the second mouse gets the cheese", and in this fast moving market, it's better to see what the competition is up to, and get the 'second mover advantage', because first movers are not always able to benefit from being first.

Whereas firms who are the first to enter the market with a new product can gain substantial market share due to lack of competition, sometimes their efforts fail. Second-mover advantage occurs when a firm who follows the lead of the first-mover is actually able to capture greater market share, despite having entered late.

First-mover firms often face high research and development costs, and the marketing costs necessary to educate the public about a new type of product. A second-mover firm can learn from the experiences of the first mover firm and may not face such high research and development costs if they are able create their own similar product using existing technology. A second-mover firm also does not face the marketing task of having to educate the public about the new project because the first mover has already done so. As a result, the second-mover can use its resources to focus on making a superior product or out-marketing the first mover.

Often second-movers are able to overwhelm first movers by taking the first-mover's product from a niche consumer market to mass markets. While firms may enjoy a first-mover advantage if they jump out to an early lead and hold onto it, the notion that winners are always the first to enter the market is a misconception. Fast Second by Costas Markides and Paul Geroski's describes this effect in further detail.

A 1993 paper by Peter N. Golder and Gerard J. Tellis describes very well what happens to startup companies entering new markets. In their analysis Golder and Tellis found almost half of the market pioneers (first movers) in their sample of 500 brands in 50 product categories failed. Even worse, the survivors' mean market share was lower than found in other studies. The issue is not being first to market, but a better understanding of the type of market your company is going to enter.

The following are a few examples of first-movers whose market share was subsequently eroded by second-movers who used their knowledge of the first entrant to build a better solution:

MySpace ~vs~ Facebook
Altavista ~vs~ Google
Netscape ~vs~ Internet Explorer
Betamax ~vs~ VHS

So just an observation: watch the hype on any predicted or new trend, sure, but don't make any wholesale changes develop a new product until you are sure you have a proven strategy or understand exactly how your customer would benefit over and above traditional methods and traditional products and are sure they will buy it.

👍 Martyn's Top Tips

- Don't jump to join new trends and create new products.
- Watch and wait – the second mouse gets the cheese.

STEP 12

GET LUCKY

Step 12

"I am a great believer in luck and I find the harder I work, the more I have of it." ~ Thomas Jefferson

He couldn't have been more correct. My own favourite saying is *"Luck is what happens when preparation meets opportunity" ~ Seneca.* We all need luck, but if you don't visualize what you want and work at it, then luck is less likely to come your way.

There was a programme on BBC many years ago that explored exactly why some people are lucky and others not so lucky. I thought it was spot on and I adopted some of the views it put forward which I am sure it made a big difference to our growth and success.

The BBC research found that luck is very much a self-fulfilling prophecy. Lucky people are more relaxed and open and therefore see what is there rather than just what they are looking for. Typically they identified four main principles:

- They are skilled at creating and noticing chance opportunities
- They make lucky decisions by listening to their intuition
- They create self-fulfilling prophesies via positive expectations
- They adopt a resilient attitude that transforms bad luck into good.

Professor Richard Wiseman, who did the study, had four top tips for becoming lucky:

- Listen to your gut instincts - they are normally right
- Be open to new experiences and breaking your normal routine
- Spend a few moments each day remembering things that went well
- Visualise yourself being lucky before an important meeting or telephone call
- So there you have it – keep things simple, focus and envisage where you want to be and it will happen.

Good luck!

GLOSSARY

accreditation: The granting of credit or recognition generally for courses

ALT tag: Used in HTML and XHTML to give alternative text – usually applies when a picture can't be seen

Amazon.com: Internet bookseller

apps: This is short of 'application' and can refer to any piece of software system and now more commonly used in reference to applications for mobile devices.

Australian PTY: Proprietary Limited Company

blog (noun): This is short for web log

blog (verb): To put things on your blog

blog post: An entry that you put on your blog

blog subscribers: People who subscribe to your blog just as they might subscribe to a magazine

blogger: Someone who blogs. For instance someone who writes articles for a blog

Blogosphere: All the blogs in the world

brand: A product, name, design or symbol that has a feature or features that separate it from others

business driver: The action that supports the company and drives business to you

buzz: The interest and conversation around a particular service or product or company

case study: An example of a principle or theory used in the practical world

cold calling: Approaching and selling to customers who are not expecting the approach

content marketing: The creation and curation of content that is disseminated to the wider audience

corridor-selling technique: Taking the customer down a corridor where there are exit doors but which you are able to pass and close through knowing and understanding what the customer is looking for

crayon rule: Where you draw a subject with a crayon and can describe your subject in three words

credit controller: Collects outstanding invoices and also extends credit

crm or customer relationship management: Management of an organisations relations and interactions with customers

crowdsourcing: The sending out of a problem to unknown solvers who then send solutions for you to choose from

curation: The gathering of content from other sources and using them, properly acknowledged, for your purposes

direct selling: Selling direct to the customer

distributor: A company or agent who supplies goods to retail outlets

domain name: Letters and numbers that make up the address for an organisation

email: Electronic mail or post

evaluation: When you send out a product for a customer to evaluate

exhibition: A display of products and services usually at a large venue

Facebook: A social networking website

Flash: An animation for web pages

font: A set of type in a particular typeface and style

forum: An internet message board

Google Adwords: A system to help you market goods and services

Google Analytics: Generates statistics about website visitors

Google Page Rank: Where a page appears on a search engine that might be based on popularity

Google: Search engine

hashtag: A tag embedded in a message on Twitter that allows people to find others with the same interests

ISBN: International Standard Book Number – a number assigned to every book before publication

keywords: Words that people type into a search engine to find products, services and ideas

lead generation: The creation or generation of prospective consumer interest or inquiry

LinkedIn Groups: The gathering together of people of similar interest in a group

LinkedIn: A business social networking site

logo: A symbol for a company

MailChimp: Used to send and collect email newsletters to subscribers

mailing list: A list of people to whom advertising is sent

mailshot: Bulk advertising

marketing led: Where a company determines what consumers want and then provides it

Meta Tag: HTML or XHTML elements

newsletter or eNewsletters: A newsletter containing information and advice to subscribers

OMIS: Overseas Market Introduction Service to help you market your business

Pareto's Law: 80% of the effects come from 20% of the causes as first discovered by Vildredo Pareto in 1906

partner: A person who shares the risks and profits with owners of a company

Passport to Export: a UK Government scheme that aims to encourage export

Pay Per Click Advertising: An advertising system used to direct people to websites

pilot: A small scale study arranged prior to launching a product or service

pin it: Button on Pinterest allows you to grab images

Pinterest: A virtual pin board

press release: A statement or document produced by an organisation for the press that discusses a particular matter that will help a company's marketing

process map: Visual representation of activities or processes

professional bodies: Non-profit organisation to which people with similar qualifications or interest belong

projectmanagement-training.com: Fictitious for the purposes of the book

QR Code: Quick response code a matrix barcode that you can scan with a smart phone

Retweet: Where someone re-posts a message on Twitter sending it on to their followers

sales cycle: The time it takes from the start of the sales process to its completion

sales lead: Someone or some company that could be interested in buying your product or service

sales-led: Where a company focuses on sales rather than marketing

Scoop.it: A simple way of producing your own curated magazine

SEO: search engine optimisation: Improving the visibility of a website without paying for it

search engine: A way of getting files, documents, photos and more from the internet

seminar: A meeting for discussion or training on a particular topic

serviced offices: Offices that provide premises and telephone answering services and other office benefits on an ad-hoc basis

SIC Code: Standard Industrial Classfication that describes the Industry Groups that companies are put into.

SIG: A special interest group is a community or group often in an organisation that focuses on and develops knowledge of a specific area

signage: Visual graphics for a specific audience

site feed: A representation of your blog that can be picked up and displayed on other websites

SlideShare: A way to upload and share slides made up of PowerPoints, Word and PDF documents

social media platform: Social media software that can be created around one profile (person, company) for marketing

social media: Social interaction via social media sites and publishing options via the internet

tag: A keyword or term used usually in computer systems

title: The title of a page

TripAdvisor: A free travel guide and research website to help people get the best deals

Twitter: Online social media networking and microblogging service

UK Trade and Industry Office: UK Government organisation promoting international trade

ukreg.co.uk: Allows you to search for domain names

URL shortening: A method of shortening URLs so that they fit on to Twitter

URL: Uniform resource locator string of characters that is a unique reference or identification code for a file available on the internet

Virtual seminar: A virtual meeting

walk-by test: Looking at something as if you were a passer-by

Web 2.0: The web as a way of sharing and participation

web cast: A media presentation on the internet

web conference: A conference on the internet

web log: The long word for blog

website: A location connected to the internet that has one or more pages that are on the Weord Wide Web

web testimonial: Online testimonial

webinar: A meeting on the internet which is attended virtually by people from anywhere in the world

Welearnmore: A fictitious company for the purposes of this book

White Paper: Authoritative report from a respected body or person

Word Tracker: Offers keyword research tools for SEO or PPC

World Wide Web: Interlinked documents accessed via the internet

YouTube: Search engine

Zulu Principle,the: Where you become in expert in one subject

INDEX

C

T

Y

Z

www.ingramcontent.com/pod-product-compliance
Lightning Source LLC
Chambersburg PA
CBHW032002170526
45157CB00002B/506